Chefs Go Wild

Chefs Go Wild

FISH AND GAME RECIPES
FROM AMERICA'S
TOP CHEFS

BY

Rebecca Gray

THE LYONS PRESS
Guilford, Connecticut
An Imprint of The Globe Pequot Press

The Lyons Press is an imprint of The Globe Pequot Press.

10 9 8 7 6 5 4 3 2 1

Printed in the United States of America

DESIGNED BY CLAIRE ZOGHB

ISBN: 1-59228-248-2

Library of Congress Cataloging-in-Publication Data is available on file.

Dedication

To the wonderful and gracious men I've consorted with over the years to find the game and create the meals: Will, Sam, Jeffrey, Alex, Hugh, Peter, P.J., Steve, Frenchy, Gordie, Charles, C.V., Wayne, Chris, Silvio, Tim, Sig, Striker, Lynn, John (times three), Dan, Roy, Jerry, and now Joe.

And always to my most important and beloved consort, Ed.

Table of Contents

Introduction

Good cookbooks have a personality. Often it comes from a straight-forward reflection of the author, a culture, or a place. If a cookbook is good and if it has character, it has gone beyond the primary purpose of instruction and moved on to entertain and inspire. And this is usually accomplished by revealing bias, passion, inspiration, humor, and probably even frailty—those human traits that combine to create an identity—and all in the context of food.

Oh, and a good cookbook does one more thing: It makes us want to cook.

When my husband, Ed, and I started *Gray's Sporting Journal* in 1975, we received, as happens to newly born magazines, a modest amount of "press." One of the standard questions asked of Ed during the interviews was why he'd started *Gray's*. His stock answer was because he wanted to read it. I think if I'd been asked that same question I'd have answered: because I wanted to write for it. I've written for many other publications now about fishing, hunting, and food and always enjoyed the process. But it was the two regular features that I did for *Gray's* that gave me the more measurable amount of continuing satisfaction and joy.

Initially I wrote biographies for *Gray's*, first under my maiden name, about people who'd managed to blend hunting and fishing into their lives on a full-time basis—guides, wildlife artists, outdoor writers, flytiers, etc. Then for many years, I either wrote the cooking feature or worked on the food photographs (or both) for *Gray's*. This background, my time with the people and wild edibles, gave focus to my innate interests, direction to my writing career, and the kind of passion that assuredly will drive the rest of my days. I've used my experiences as a kind of glue in this book, pulling together these wonderful chefs in the camaraderie of what it is to cook from the wild. I hope for you it is as if we are all sitting around my table, enjoying the company and the food and discussing our day in the field and in the kitchen—and the joy of bringing it to the table.

This is my seventh or eighth—depending on how you count a paperback edition—cookbook. Most are collections of recipes on preparing fish or game, or both, all include in varying degrees people who are enthusiastic foodies. *Chefs Go Wild* conceptually continues the trend, combining the *Gray's* game food features with the biographies.

However, there is something different about this particular book, and it comes out of what has happened over the past couple of decades to the acceptance and definition of "wild" foods. In the late 1970s and into the early 1980s, it was a rare restaurant that served any type of game. A specialty store might carry an occasional farm-raised quail, pheasant, or rabbit, but again it was unusual. Of course, the laws prevented any hunted species from being sold, so the rarity of game was partially due to lack of supply, but clearly also lack of demand. Yet as I can attest to—so do Joe Messina (see p. 132) and Michael Gray (no relation to me) (see p. 47)—it all began to change in the 1990s. Quite suddenly game became very popular. I have speculated about why this happened and have many theories: the health benefits of fatless game; the movement toward organic, chemically untampered-with meats; increased interest and support of local foods; and the fact that eating game can be kind of titillating and thrilling. But I wondered, was game now being served by chefs in search of a new star on the culinary stage with which to impress their worldly and increasingly knowledgeable clientele? There are, I'm sure, many other plausible reasons for the game boom.

As a hunter and game cook, I was at first slightly annoyed, even arrogant, about *faux* wild game. In my mind, the game farms and their homogenized pen-raised birds couldn't stand up to the real thing. Only birds feeding on worms, twigs, wild berries, and the like, shot and then field-dressed by my own hand—or a friend's—counted as wild in my books. Then in 1998, I wrote a book about venison and used farm-raised cuts supplied by D'Artagnan's (see p. 15) for the photos. The photographer, a woman-friend named Christopher Hirsheimer, was also an editor of the food magazine *SAVEUR* and a very accomplished cook. Together we cooked and styled the shots and then ate the venison; it was delicious. And the "aha" here was that it was available on demand, not just the year that Ed shot a deer!

The other aspect that mellowed my incredulity over the ever-evolving definition of game came about when I started writing a column for *Shooting Sportsman* magazine. For the column, I wrote about professional chefs—usually hunters themselves—who featured game on their menus. (The columns actually became the basis for this book.) I discovered that for most of these chefs wild was a broad and evocative descriptor, not a technical term.

There *is* a difference, and all who cook game know it, and I will always have my bias. But what farm-raised game allows for is a perpetuation of the culinary sensibilities that are inherent in cooking truly wild game. Cooking game—wild or not—is interesting, often challenging, exciting, founded in culinary history, and can provide an intensely connected experience in eating that we can't get from grocery store beef or chicken. This blended wildness is perfectly acceptable, and how much a chef cooks with the real wild stuff doesn't really matter.

I did discover an interesting link between the wild chefs portrayed here and those of us devoted to the natural world. We share a common attitude. Qualities that I had at one time reserved just for hunters and fishermen—independence, a sense of adventure, a bit of wanderlust, and very often a touch of exuberance—seem to be represented in a good game chef, too. And does this outlook transfer to their style and cuisine? I think so.

This time, in this book, I rely heavily on describing the lives, history, and character of those whose livelihood is food-based. Why do that, devote pages of words in a cookbook to describing the chefs? Why not just write down the recipes? Because the who and where and what of a recipe give the dish context and provide a kind of reliability and assurance. Knowing that a recipe was concocted by someone who comes from Quebec or Vermont; that they are Mexican American, Native American, or of Italian descent; if they were formally trained in the culinary arts; or if their jobs require cooking game nearly every day—all of those credentials tell you something about their recipes and speak to your willingness to invest in them.

In this day of spending less and less time on meal preparation, let's use the clues to prioritize how to spend time and energy. If you crave game prepared Mexican-American style, stop, do not read further, go directly to Jesse Perez (see p. 185). Or if you enjoy the complexities of ingredients and technique from a lifelong professional chef, jump to the section on Wayne Nish (see p. 171) or Charlie van Over and Priscilla Martel (see p. 208). Or for someone who cooks wild game every single day in season, try Francine Forrester (see p. 28) or Afif Espindola (see p. 8). Of course, I could go on and on—and I do! Also, I suspect once you have read this book you will be able to do the reverse: read a recipe and know about the person who created it. Why include the chef biographies? They give the book personality—or actually personalities—and really, really entertain.

This book is about people whose lives are defined by a love of good food. And they have to some extent all bared a bit of their souls by letting me reproduce their stories and recipes here. Or, as is explained so clearly in those often repeated words from the nineteenth century writer, Jean-Anthelme Brillat-Savarin: "Tell me what you eat and I'll tell you who you are." Did they know what they were doing when they gave me their recipes? Perhaps not, but then they were, to a person, very generous with me, and I thank them.

My mom, when asked which of her three children is her favorite, always replies, "The child who's with me." Even though my sister and I know the real answer is our brother, I understand what she means. As I interviewed the chefs, tested the recipes, and wrote about the chefs included here, each one passed through a time of being my favorite. But in the end they are, of course, all my favorite. I am very happy to know them, to display their expertise, and to pass it all along to you.

So welcome to my album, my collection of culinary wild men and women snapshots. May you read, learn, have fun, and most of all, return to your kitchen with renewed joy.

Sammy Citrano

Restaurant Owner and Cook,
George's and Coffee Shop Café
Waco and McGregor, Texas

Sammy Citrano is like no other chef in this book. In fact, the first thing he said to me was, "I'm no chef. I cook, and I own restaurants, but I'm no chef." But Sammy is included here for a good reason: He cooks good food, as he says, "Comfort food. I use simple recipes and cook it right." And he comes from a part of the world—Texas—where nearly everyone has hunted or fished at least once in their lives and most main course recipes probably started as a fish or game recipe. It's a part of the world where dove is interchangeable with chicken (unless you intend to sell it) and where game can be nothing special. There are times when that's important. And I can remember a time when a little less making the game special, a little less celebration of it, would have been very good.

I was in New Brunswick, Canada, on the last day of our annual woodcock hunt, the final hours of our weeklong trip, and the morning after our end-of-the-hunt, celebratory game dinner. After hours, we commandeered the kitchen of the inn where we were staying; I cooked dinner, which always included woodcock and crème brûlée, for the twelve of us. The eleven men in the hunting party sous-chefed—cleaned birds and made salad—and kept themselves and the cook well supplied with vodka martinis. That night was great fun—full of many bottles of wine, lots of toasts, Cohibas, and laughing and not a whole lot of sleep. The next day was not all that much fun. We hurt. Every time we emerged from the car to hunt a woodcock covert, I wore my sunglasses, despite the overcast day, and said a little prayer asking that the opportunity to fire my gun never present itself—shooting would be way too loud. Not surprisingly, the morning hunt proved unproductive, and we were now traveling to our afternoon set of coverts when suddenly one of my hunting companions, Peter Macy, cried, "Wait! Stop. Go back to that roadside take-out place."

We made a U-turn and came to rest before the window of the little joint, and then I smelled it. Definitely onion rings. Peter was just like a bird dog on point when it came to onion rings. We ordered up big, juicy cheeseburgers with bacon—some of us had more than two—multiple containers of huge, crispy rings, the onion still piping hot inside the crust, and Cokes all around. The food did the trick. Something about the fat, the protein, the fat, the bread, the caffeine, and well, the fat proved a different kind of hair-of-the-dog for what ailed us. This simple, basic, made-to-order lunch was a good antidote to the excesses and was the ultimate comfort food.

Our game dinners on our New Brunswick hunts are always memorable, but when Peter and I see each other now we always return, not to the meal of woodcock encrusted in juniper berries with the beach plum cream sauce, but to those cheeseburgers and onion rings. There are just times when plain food is the best. But I've also thought that game could, should, hold that ordinary status, too. Is it realistic or critical to the success of the meal to always make game into something special, a ceremonious event? Wouldn't the ultimate be to have so much fish and game in your life that it was regularly your comfort food? But would we be prepared? Would there be "the simple recipes to cook it right"? I went looking.

Of course, I started my search in Texas where more venison meat is processed each year than any other state and where eating fish and game is as common as fried and barbecue ribs. I found Sammy Citrano, who happens at times to cook for the most famous hunter in Texas, George W. Bush. The Bush ranch is in Crawford, a tiny town 30 minutes or so west of Waco. President Bush gets a lot of his food catered into the ranch, not just for the family, but for the press corps, Air Force One personnel, and White House staff who accompany him. And the man who does the catering—and also owns the nearest restaurant, the Coffee Shop Café in neighboring McGregor—is Sammy Citrano.

Born in Beaumont, Texas, Sammy says he first got interested in cooking when he took a home economics course in high school. But he'd started in the food *business* long before that, when he was ten years old. Sammy's Aunt Katie made sandwiches for grocery stores. Sammy and a group of his lady relatives then took the fresh sandwiches to the stores and brought back the day-old ones and fed them to the hogs.

Sammy is a second generation Italian-Sicilian on both sides. Most of his family lived in Texas when he was growing up, and big meals, often with 20 or more relatives and guests, were part of everyday life. Meal preparation was non-stop. And with no convenience foods—Sammy recalls his mother grating Parmesan by wrapping the cheese in cloth and rubbing it—cooking was an all-day affair. As a kid, Sammy hunted squirrel and deer on his cousin's few acres that were used usually for grazing cattle. He and his dad shrimped and caught crab over on the Gulf, too. Food was always a part of his life.

During college, Sammy lived with a group of guys who'd bought a rental property together, actually an old church, and rented out rooms to students. There was no kitchen in the building, so the mothers of the students made big lasagnas to take each week to their kids. There was an opportunity here: Sammy and his buddies put in a kitchen, then a bar, and Sammy was managing his first restaurant. Then Sammy moved across town to work at the Steak and Spirit, and his restaurant career was truly launched. By the time Sammy was twenty-five years old, he was president of a restaurant chain that had five stores and employed five hundred people.

In 1981, Sammy married Delonda ("The best cook I know," says Sammy), and in 1985, the Citranos moved to Waco to become part owners of the Elite Café. By 1993, they'd bought into George's—previously known as Harry B's, it had been a restaurant since the 1930s—right next to Baylor University. And by 1998, they had full ownership of George's and purchased the Coffee Shop Café. Both Citrano restaurants have menus with great comfort food items: Texas Toothpicks (fried onion and jalapeño strips), Crab Toasts (Delonda's spicy concoction), Cajun Fried Crawfish Tails, and their signature drink the Big O (18-ounce draft beers in a fishbowl glass).

The Crazy Wings are my personal favorite. Originally made with that nearly pestilent bird the mourning dove, at the restaurants it's made with chicken tenders. The breast meat surrounds a cube of Monterey Jack and a pickled jalapeño slice. This is wrapped in bacon and deep-fat fried. Yes, this is definitely a dish I could call comfort food. Now if I could just figure out a way to make woodcock as plentiful as dove, this could add a whole new concept to our New Brunswick game dinners.

Seafood Gabrielle

(SERVES 2)

3 tablespoons dry white wine

2 tablespoons unsalted butter

1/8 cup lemon juice

3 tablespoons extra virgin olive oil

3 teaspoons Gabrielle Seasoning* or herb mixture of basil, thyme, rosemary, and oregano

1/2 pound redfish or any firm-flesh fish (such as catfish) or Texas Gulf Coast shrimp, cut into 4 pieces

Combine the wine, butter, lemon juice and oil in a frying pan. Over low heat, melt the butter and bring to simmer. Let simmer and don't let boil for a few minutes and then stir in the Gabrielle Seasoning. Add the fish pieces and poach in the liquid for 6 to 8 minutes (if using shrimp, cook only 4 to 5 minutes). Remove the fish to plates and pour the remaining sauce over fish.

This is delicious served with crusty bread.

*Available by mail order from thechef@chefgeof.com

George's Little O Doe

(SERVES 2)

1 tablespoon olive oil

3 tablespoons butter

6 ounces venison tenderloin, sliced into medallions

Spicet* or seasoning salt

Gabrielle Seasoning* or herb mixture of basil, thyme, rosemary, and
    oregano

6 mushrooms, sliced

3 artichoke hearts, sliced into 8–10 pieces

2 green onions or scallions, sliced

1 medium garlic clove, chopped

2 teaspoons fresh parsley, chopped

Several drops Worcestershire sauce

Sprig fresh parsley

    In a 10-inch skillet, heat the oil and 1 tablespoon of the butter. Season the venison with Spicet and Gabrielle Seasoning and place the medallions on one side of the skillet. On the other side, put the mushrooms, artichoke hearts, green onions or scallions, garlic, and 1 teaspoon of the chopped parsley. Cook for 3 minutes, moving the vegetables and turning the venison. After 3 more minutes, remove the venison. Add the remaining chopped parsley and the Worcestershire sauce. Season to taste with a little more Spicet and Gabrielle Seasoning. Fold in the remaining butter. Ladle the sauce on top of the venison medallions and add the sprig of parsley.

*Available by mail order from thechef@chefgeof.com

Crazy Wings

(MAKES 12)

6 dove, breasted, or 12 1/2 ounces chicken tenders
12 1/2-inch cubes Monterey Jack cheese
2–3 pickled jalapeños, sliced into 12 pieces
12 bacon slices
Oil for deep frying (optional)

Pound each of the 12 dove breasts until they are the size of your first two fingers put together. Wrap a cube of cheese and a slice of pickled jalapeño with each dove breast. Now wrap each dove/cheese ball in bacon, wrapping one way around, and then the other way around so the breast is completely covered by the bacon.

Place the wings in a baking dish. Set them in the freezer for about 1 hour.

Preheat the oven to 350 degrees. Remove the wings from the freezer and bake for 25 to 30 minutes. (The wings can now be refrigerated or frozen until ready for the final cooking.)

In a deep-fat fryer in the oil—or, if you prefer, on a grill—cook the wings for 8 minutes. Drain on paper towels.

I serve these Crazy Wings with ranch dressing.

Afif Espindola

Chef, Rock Springs Ranch
Paicines, California

"Cooking game completes the hunting process for me; it brings the harvesting full circle," Afif Espindola explains. Afif is the chef at the Rock Springs Ranch in Paicines, California, an elegant guest ranch located on 19,000 acres just three hours south of the San Francisco airport. The ranch is often host to the California Side by Side Society gatherings because its nine-month hunting season focuses predominantly on bird hunting—from dove, to both bobwhite and the native California quail, then chukar and Hungarian partridge, and pheasant in March—with black-tailed deer and wild boar filling in the hunting year in May and June. Afif's hunting and cooking—both introduced early in his life—have culminated into a wonderful knowledge; and for the twelve guests at the Ranch, his fine culinary skills certainly round out and complete their hunting experience.

Born in Ecuador to parents of Ecuadorian, Spanish, and Italian descent, Afif immigrated to the United States as a small boy. The family moved frequently—mostly throughout the Midwest—and Afif recalls one of his first hunts was for Kansas pheasants. He remembers, too, his grandmother who determined the age and condition of a chicken—when it was still possible to buy a chicken in the feathers—by examining the feet.

Afif's career track as a professional chef began in 1977 with a three-year apprenticeship in the kitchens of Swiss Chalet in Woodland Park, Colorado.

A series of training situations through the American Culinary Federation followed and—as is characteristic of many professional chefs—a vagabond existence of moving from one culinary venue to another—from the Baltimore and Broadmoor hotels to work on a cruise line, then two years in St. Thomas and St. John in the Caribbean. At each place, Afif picked up on the proficiencies of others—whether pastry from the Austrian chefs of the Virgin Island hotels or the mentoring influence of his first teacher, Hans Peter Haas, at the Swiss Chalet. And Afif developed his own expertise in pâtés and galantines for the grand buffets. But by the late 1980s, grand buffets were a fading element in commercial dining rooms—and ground and forced meats, with their heavy fat content, were less popular, too—plus there was little time or place for Afif to hunt.

Then, almost fortuitously, a back injury—which meant the physical demands of a large kitchen became formidable—forced Afif to consider an alternative situation. The small, intimate dining room of Rock Springs Ranch, coupled with time off to hunt and a place to kennel a bird dog, was obviously appealing to him. But the frosting on the cake had to have been the wild chukar partridge.

"I love chukar, both to hunt and cook," Afif said. "I like to hunt anything that involves dog work—ducks, quail—and I take annual trips to Oregon and Nevada for Huns and grouse, but I love the chukars."

Afif's signature recipe is Marinated Breasts of Chukar: first marinate chukar in honey, brown sugar, fresh herbs, balsamic vinegar, and Dijon mustard and then cook for 4 to 5 minutes and sauce with stock made from the chukar bones.

"I never breast-out a bird in the field, even if the recipe only calls for just breast meat," Afif said. "I want the bones to make a good stock for the sauce."

There is time, too, at Rock Springs for other than hunting. Afif makes longbows by hand, attends Western Rendezvous where he teaches arrowhead making, learns to tan leather in the old tradition, and laments, "I was definitely born a hundred years too late." Perhaps from a hunting standpoint, but as far as cooking is concerned, I'm happy Afif is part of the twenty-first century.

Marinated Breasts of Chukar with Chanterelles

(SERVES 6)

1 bunch parsley or small bunch cilantro

6 garlic cloves

2–3 shallots

1/2 cup orange juice

1/4 cup balsamic vinegar

1/4 cup honey

1/4 cup soy sauce

2 tablespoons brown sugar

3 tablespoons Dijon mustard

1 1/2–2 cups olive oil

6–8 chukars or quail

Salt

Pepper

1/4 cup white wine

4 tablespoons butter

2 shallots, finely chopped

1/2 pound fresh chanterelles or other wild mushroom, cleaned and chopped

1 cup Homemade Game Stock (see recipe below)

In a food processor or blender, combine the cilantro, cloves, 2–3 shallots, orange juice, vinegar, honey, soy sauce, sugar, and mustard and pulse to process. Then slowly add the oil until the mixture is emulsified. The marinade should be strong tasting and on the sweet side. If it is too sweet, add a bit more soy sauce.

Bone the chukar breasts whole and reserve the carcass and legs for the stock. Lightly pound the breasts to flatten slightly and place in the marinade for at least 12 hours.

Season the chukar breasts with salt and pepper. In a hot skillet with a little oil, brown the flattened breasts quickly and remove to a heated platter. Deglaze the pan with the wine, scraping the remaining breast bits with a whisk. Add the butter and shallots and cook until translucent. Add the chanterelle mushrooms and cook for 5 minutes or so over high heat. Add the stock and reduce. The sauce can be tightened with a roux or left au jus. Return the breasts to the hot skillet, cover, and let cook off the heat for about 1 minute. Serve immediately.

■ ■ ■

Homemade Game Stock

Bones and legs from chukars (see above)
1 tablespoon olive oil
1 onion, sliced
1/2 bunch celery, chopped
2 carrots, chopped
6–8 cups water

Preheat the oven to 450 degrees. Put the bones in a roasting pan and drizzle with the oil. Place in the preheated oven to brown. In a separate pan, place the onion, celery, and carrots and roast until well done and there is a wonderful aroma. Combine the vegetables with the bones, add enough water to cover the bones, and bring to a boil on top of the stove. Reduce the liquid to about half or until it tastes like a well-flavored stock. Strain and refrigerate the stock.

Marinated Breasts of Chukar with Apricot Sauce

(SERVES 4)

4 chukar, plucked and cleaned
3 tablespoons brown sugar
1 cup mayonnaise
3 garlic cloves
1/4 cup balsamic vinegar
1/4 cup orange juice
1 bunch fresh herbs (thyme, basil, rosemary)
1/2 cup olive oil
Pepper
Salt
Apricot Sauce (see recipe below)

Cut the breast meat off of each bird, leaving as much skin on as possible (Save the remaining carcasses for making game stock.) Purée the brown sugar, mayonnaise, cloves, vinegar, orange juice, fresh herbs, and oil in a blender or food processor. Pepper the breasts and place them in a bowl with the marinade for 4 to 6 hours. Remove to a plate, leaving the thick marinade mixture on top of the breasts and reserve the liquid for the Apricot Sauce.

Heat a skillet with no oil. Salt the chukar breasts. Do not remove the excess marinade. Sear the chukar skin-side down for 2 1/2 minutes on each side. Divide the Apricot Sauce (see recipe below) equally among 4 warmed plates. Remove the chukar from the skillet and place each breast on a sauced plate.

Apricot Sauce

1/4 cup white wine
Reserved liquid (see above)
5 tablespoons unsalted butter
1 shallot, finely chopped
2 tablespoons sugar
1/4 cup apricot jam
1/4 cup game stock, dark in color (see Homemade Game Stock on p. 11)
2 tablespoons Dijon mustard
Salt
Pepper

Using the skillet that the chukar breasts were cooked in, deglaze the skillet with the wine and half the reserved liquid. Add 2 tablespoons of the butter to the skillet and sauté the shallots briefly. Sprinkle the shallots with the sugar and cook until caramelized and then deglaze with the remaining reserved liquid. Add the apricot jam and stock and allow to cook down. Add the mustard and do not allow it to boil. Add salt and pepper to taste and remove from the heat. Swirl in the remaining butter.

Braised Rabbit

(SERVES 6 TO 8)

Salt
Pepper
3–4 cottontail rabbits, legs removed and carcasses reserved
1/4 cup peanut oil
Flour
1 cup white wine
1 tablespoon butter
3 shallots, finely chopped
3 garlic cloves, finely chopped
1/4 cup honey
1 cup tomato juice
Rabbit stock, or good beef stock, to cover
1 bay leaf

Salt and pepper the rabbit thighs. Heat the oil in a skillet. Dust the rabbit thighs with flour. Sear the rabbit thighs over high heat, turning until brown on all sides and then remove from the skillet.

Deglaze the skillet with the wine, then remove the liquid and reserve. Add the butter to the skillet and sauté the shallots and garlic briefly. Add the reserved liquid and deglaze. Add the honey, tomato juice, bay leaf, and stock and bring to a slight simmer. Add the rabbit thighs, legs, and carcasses, cover, and cook gently for 3 to 4 hours or until the meat is tender. Remove the meat and bay leaf and increase the heat. Cook the liquid down until thick. Season with salt and pepper to taste and return the rabbit meat to the sauce.

George Faison

Co-owner, D'Artagnan's and Game Purveyors
Newark, New Jersey

"The meat of the woodcock is the only terrestrial food of the gods." The quote from the cook Elzéar Blaze—and recorded by Alexandre Dumas—introduces the chapter on grouse and woodcock in George Faison and Ariane Daguin's cookbook, *D'Artagnan's Glorious Game Cookbook* (Little Brown, 1999*)*. George and Ariane are partners in the twenty-year-old company, D'Artagnan's, the foremost purveyor of game and exotic meats in the United States, supplying primarily to restaurants, specialty stores, and supermarkets. The inclusion of Blaze's exaltation, indeed the very mention of woodcock in their book, is particularly interesting because woodcock is a game bird that they can not sell.

George Faison grew up in Houston, Texas, and was introduced to game as a nine-year-old boy hunting dove and quail. In 1981, he attended New York's Columbia University for his MBA. There he met undergraduate Ariane Daguin, a native of Gascony—the region in France where, as she aptly puts it: "[Moulard ducks and foie gras] are the backbone of gastronomic tradition. For local inhabitants, there is almost a religious reverence about the birds." And Ariane's father André Daguin, chef-owner of Hôtel de France in Auch is renowned for his rare-cooked *magrets*, the breasts of fatted Moulard ducks.

In 1983, virtually all foie gras in the United States was imported and supplies were limited to canned rather than fresh foie gras. The same year, the local Texas economy was mired in recession. These two seemingly unrelated conditions combined to present a business opportunity for George and Ariane: For George there was no impetus to return to Houston's high unemployment market; he'd spent time in France and now held a business degree. For Ariane her family background had brought her consulting relationships to the burgeoning U.S. foie gras market. Initial employment at *Les Trois Petits Cochon*, a producer of foie gras in New York City, was a natural first step for both of them. But when some restaurateurs and chefs refused to work with the U.S.-based producer of foie gras, entrepreneurship and a partnership beckoned George and Ariane to fill a niche.

George and Ariane started D'Artagnan's in 1984, and they quickly realized that if they limited their product line to foie gras they "were going to starve" or at least have nothing to eat but a lot of duck livers—not a bad way to go. They decided adding fresh game to the offerings was healthier on many levels.

"Initially, as well as now, finding quality sources for game has been the most challenging part of the business," George recounted. "That, and building the demand."

In 1984, rabbit was generally supplied frozen to a very few restaurants and usually ended up being fed to the kitchen staff for dinner.

"Now we're selling five thousand fresh rabbits a week," George said. (Although in 2002 the brown hare was on the embargo list due to mad cow disease.) And, of course, a lot of other game species, too—everything from quail and pheasant to boar, buffalo, and venison, even some of the truly wild species such as Scottish grouse, red-legged partridge, and brown hare—can be had from D'Artagnan's.

And then there are the exotics. Virtually all exotic meat is, or was at some time, actually game somewhere in the world, but by virtue of limited availability and/or taboos within a particular culture, the meat crosses into the exotic category. Exotic foods often smack of the strange, and are an acquired taste and very much on the edge of acceptability, more so than game. Game and exotic meats can both maintain a position at the pinnacle of what is considered gourmet and trendy—or not.

My first "or not" encounter with an edible exotic fortunately didn't involve any pressure to actually eat it. I was not an unusually tall child but tall enough at the age of eight to be able to clearly see what was on the tippy-top shelf of the pantry closet. There, wedged amongst the Campbell's soup cans, was a very large glass jar containing a huge eyeball nearly the dimension of my entire child-size head. It stared blankly out into the upper echelons of the closet space, waiting, evidently, for its turn in the pot. This chance meeting with a whale's eye—sent to my dad by fellow meatpackers—happened in the 1950s, long before "Save the Whales" was relevant.

Both George and Ariane are quick to point out the restrictions in their game and exotic meat business: Logically any sale of parts from endangered species is forbidden; additionally, laws prohibit the import of migratory birds or animals indigenous to North America. D'Artagnan's may sell rattlesnake or alligator readily. But if a request for lion loin came in, it would be politely explained that although legal, only meat from a zoo lion, frozen after it had died presumably of old age, could be obtained.

When asked what the most difficult to obtain ingredient is, George replies unhesitatingly, "Blood. The chefs request it and need it for saucing game [used either as is or as an ingredient in sauce recipes], but it's very difficult to get and requires buying multiples of the specific game."

So with a multitude of hunted species and exotics available to him, what is George's favorite?

"To hunt and then to eat what is *truly* wild, what is sincerely wily and not just scared," George said. "Woodcock is the very best." Ah, the mystery of the Dumas/Blaze quote and inclusion of woodcock in George's book is explained.

Of course, that which can not be had easily is often most coveted. But then again many of us—cooks, hunters, and game purveyors—believe as Blaze in the heavenly flavor of woodcock. And despite its rarity and its wild and cunning nature, I've yet to find such adulation of a whale's eyeball.

Roasted Woodcock with Pancetta, Armagnac, and Cream

(SERVES 4 AS A MAIN COURSE)

4 woodcocks
Salt
Black pepper
12 slices French bread
1 pound Grade B foie gras cut into 3/4-inch cubes
1/2 cup finely chopped onion
8 thin slices pancetta, chopped fine
1/2 cup Armagnac
1 cup heavy cream
1 cup duck and veal demi-glace

Preheat the oven to 450 degrees. If necessary, pluck the woodcock and remove entrails (leave the heads on). Discard the gizzards and set the remaining giblets and entrails aside. Blot the woodcock dry with paper towels. Season the woodcocks inside and out with salt and pepper. Stuff the cavity of each with 1 slice of bread and a few cubes of foie gras. Truss the cavities using the birds' beaks. Set aside.

Heat a heavy skillet over high heat. Add the remaining foie gras, 1/4 cup of the onion, and the pancetta to the skillet and quickly sauté just until onions are lightly colored, about 2 minutes. Remove the mixture from skillet with a slotted spoon and reserve. Still over heat, add the reserved giblets and entrails and the remaining 1/4 cup of onion, stirring until the onion softens and a paste forms. Season with salt and pepper.

Keep warm. Toast the remaining slices of bread and spread with the onion mixture.

Heat the same skillet and brown the woodcock briefly on top of stove, then bake in the preheated oven for 7 to 8 minutes. Remove, transfer to a plate, untruss, and let rest. Return the reserved foie gras, onion, and pancetta mixture to pan. Pour in the Armagnac, scraping up any browned cooking bits, then add the cream, demi-glace, and salt and pepper to taste. Bring to a boil and cook until thickened into a sauce. Serve 1 woodcock on each plate, garnished with 2 slices of the toast and the sauce.

Note: This recipe was adapted from Kirk Avondoglio, executive chef-owner, Perona Farms, Andover, New Jersey, and included in D'Artagnan's Glorious Game Cookbook, Little Brown *(October, 1999).*

Southwestern Venison Kebabs with Tomato Salsa

(SERVES 4 GENEROUSLY)

Note: For this dish, you'll need 8 bamboo skewers, soaked overnight in water.

3 Yukon Gold potatoes, peeled and cut into 1- by 2-inch pieces

2–3 tablespoons olive oil

8 medium-large white mushrooms, stems trimmed, wiped, and cut in half

Rice

Tomato Salsa (see recipe below)

4 1/2 pounds venison, cut from leg, well trimmed, and cut into 1- by 2-inch pieces

1 green bell pepper, cut lengthwise into 1-inch strips

1 yellow bell pepper, cut lengthwise into 1-inch strips

46 cherry tomatoes

Salt

Black pepper

1/3 cup ancho chile paste

Cover the potatoes with cold water in a saucepan. Bring the water to a boil and cook for 10 minutes. Drain and plunge the potatoes into very cold water to stop cooking. Blot the potatoes dry with paper towels and reserve.

Heat 1 tablespoon of the oil in a skillet over high heat. Add the mushrooms and sauté until lightly colored but still firm inside, about 4 to 5 minutes, shaking pan to turn and cook evenly.

Light a gas or charcoal grill and heat until medium-hot. Or heat a broiler. Prepare the rice according to package directions. Prepare the Tomato Salsa (see recipe below).

Thread the venison, peppers, mushrooms, tomatoes, and potatoes onto skewers. Brush each with a little of the remaining olive oil, season with salt and pepper, and brush on the ancho chile paste. Grill until the meat is rare or medium-rare, about 2 to 3 minutes per side.

Spoon a mound of rice onto 4 plates. Add a generous amount of Tomato Salsa and 2 kebabs per plate.

∎ ∎ ∎

Tomato Salsa

1 can (28-ounce) crushed tomatoes
2–3 tablespoons chopped cilantro leaves
2 jalapeños, seeds and membranes removed, chopped
2 tablespoons ground cumin
1 bunch scallions, chopped
1 red onion, chopped
1 tablespoon minced garlic
Lime juice
Salt
Black pepper

Combine the tomatoes, cilantro, jalapeños, cumin, scallions, red onion, and garlic in an electric blender or food processor and purée until almost smooth. Season with lime juice, salt, and pepper to taste.

Duck Magret with Mole and Mango Salsa
(SERVES FOUR)

This wonderful recipe contrasts the unctuous rich flavor of the duck with the exotic and spicy flavor of the mole and the vibrant tropical fruit salsa. The mole, while complex, is not "hot" and the salsa provides a refreshing acidity due to the addition of lime juice. The mole requires some work but can be prepared days ahead and frozen. The recipe here will make enough for several meals and goes well with venison, tuna, and all poultry.

Mole

4 ancho chiles

3 mulato chiles

3 guajillo chiles

2 pasillas chiles

2 chipotle chiles*

3 tablespoons sesame seeds

7 tablespoons duck fat (any fat will do)

1 2-inch piece cinnamon stick, ground

5 cloves, ground

5 black peppercorns, ground

1 chopped onion

7 cloves garlic, minced

3 tomatoes, chopped (drained canned ones work best in winter)

1 small plantain, chopped

1 bunch fresh thyme and 6 sprigs oregano tied together

1/3 cup dark raisins

3/4 cup blanched almonds

6 cups duck stock or chicken stock

1 thick slice of day old brioche or hallah bread crushed into fine crumbs (about 1 cup)

2 ounces grated Mexican chocolate or very dark richly flavored chocolate

Salt

Wash and dry all the chiles and then remove the tops, seeds, and veins. Soak the chiles together in a bowl covered with warm water for about 30 minutes. Then drain them in a colander but save 1 to 2 cups of the liquid in case you need to thin out the sauce.

In a skillet, cook the sesame seeds until just golden brown and place them in a small bowl.

In a large skillet, heat 3 tablespoons of the fat until sizzling. Add the cinnamon, cloves, and peppercorns and cook, stirring, for 2 minutes. Then add the onion, garlic, tomatoes, plantain, the bunch of thyme and oregano, toasted sesame seeds, raisins, and almonds. Cook for 15 minutes, uncovered and stirring frequently. Remove the thyme and oregano.

Let this mixture cool for 15 minutes, then place half of the mixture in a food processor with 1 cup of the stock and half the drained chiles. Process until really smooth, about 3 minutes. Repeat with the remaining mixture and chiles.

In a large pot, heat the remaining 4 tablespoons of fat until sizzling and slowly add the chile puree. Stir well and frequently. Slowly add the remaining 4 cups of stock, adding more as it is absorbed by the mixture. Then cook covered for 15 minutes, stirring. Stir in the bread crumbs and cook another 10 minutes, then add the chocolate and cook another 5 minutes. Last but not least, season with salt to taste.

All the chiles are dried and readily available in most markets these days. If you cannot find all these chiles don't worry. But the ancho is imperative. It is the sweet raisiny one that balances all the others.

. . .

Mango Salsa

2 ripe mangos, peeled, sliced lengthwise and chopped into 1/2-inch
    cubes
2 small shallots, chopped
2 serrano chiles, chopped
1 yellow bell pepper, chopped
1 red bell pepper, chopped
2–3 tablespoons cilantro, chopped
2 tablespoons olive oil
Juice of 1–2 limes
Sea salt

In a bowl, toss the mangos, shallots, chiles, peppers, and cilantro together. Add the oil and lime juice. Season to taste with sea salt. (If the
salsa needs more acidity, add more lime juice. If you want more of a specific color, add more of that particular vegetable. If you want more heat,
add another serrano chile.)

. . .

Duck Breasts

4 duck breasts*

Preheat the oven to 350 degrees. Place the duck breast in a baking
dish. Bake the duck breasts in the oven for 30 minutes, or until a meat

thermometer inserted into the center of the breast registers 120 to 125 degrees. Let the duck rest lightly covered for 5 to 10 minutes prior to slicing. Score the skin of the breasts and slowly render any fat, skin side down. (This is not necessary for wild ducks unless you perceive the need.) Finish the breasts on the grill, in the oven, or on the stovetop by quickly cooking for just a few minutes until the skin is golden brown.

* The duck breast in the recipe is the breast of the foie gras duck, a.k.a. magret. Any duck breast domesticated or wild can be used. In fact wild ducks or geese work best because their fuller flavor balances better with the other components. As for cooking, the breast is best served medium rare.

■ ■ ■

To Serve

Spoon the salsa on the top half of the plate. Slice the duck breast and put 5 to 6 slices over the center of each portion of salsa leaving salsa showing at the top. Then top the bottom of the duck breast with the mole covering the bottom portion of the plate. The colors and flavors are sensational.

This dish goes great with a rich fruity Zinfandel or Syrah.

Red Snapper and Foie Gras with Artichokes and Black Truffle Sauce

(SERVES 4)

Salt

Juice of 1 lemon

1 tablespoon extra virgin olive oil

4 large artichokes

1 ounce black truffles (melanosporum only: fresh, frozen, or canned)

1/2 cup duck and veal demi-glace

1/2 cup truffle juice (melanosporum only)

1/2 cup shrimp stock or clam broth

4 tablespoons unsalted butter, cut in pieces

2 ounces cold foie gras terrine, cut in pieces

4 slices fresh foie gras, 1/2-inch wide, about 2 ounces each

4 fillets of red snapper, skinless (8 ounces each)

Good quality sea salt

White pepper

1 tablespoon balsamic vinegar

1 tablespoon canola oil

Bring a large saucepan of salted water to a boil. Add the lemon juice and olive oil. Stem the artichokes, cut off leaves, and trim around hearts. Cook the hearts in the saucepan until tender, about 30 minutes. Set the hearts aside to cool in liquid. (The recipe can be made to this point up to 1 day ahead, but refrigerate the artichokes in their liquid.) Use a spoon to scoop the chokes out of the artichoke hearts and cut the hearts into pie-shaped wedges, 1/2-inch at the thickest part. Set aside.

Cut half of the truffle into julienne and finely chop the rest. Set aside.

Combine the demi-glace, truffle juice, and shrimp stock or clam broth in a medium saucepan and bring it to a simmer over medium heat. Adjust the heat down so the liquid is just below a simmer. Whisking constantly, gradually add the butter and foie gras terrine. Strain the mixture through a fine mesh sieve into another saucepan. Stir in the chopped truffle and set aside. (The recipe can be made to this point the morning before serving, but cover and refrigerate the sauce.)

Season the foie gras slices and snapper fillets on both sides with salt and pepper. Place a 10-inch skillet over high heat until it is very hot. Put the foie gras slices in the skillet and sear until browned, about 30 seconds per side. Remove the foie gras from the skillet and keep warm. Put the artichoke pieces in the skillet along with the balsamic vinegar and sauté them until lightly browned, about 1 minute. Remove and keep the artichokes warm. In a larger skillet heat the canola oil until quite hot, then add the fish and cook until done, about 7 minutes on the first side, 3 or 4 on the flip side.

To assemble, ladle a spoonful of sauce on each plate and place a snapper fillet and slice of foie gras on the sauce. Top with artichoke pieces and the julienne truffle and serve.

Francine Forrester

Chef, Bighorn River Resort
Fort Smith, Montana

Nick and Francine Forrester own and operate the Bighorn River Resort just north of Fort Smith, Montana, overlooking the Bighorn River. The area is, of course, best known to sportsmen for its gold-medal trout waters. But Nick is a wildlife biologist with specific expertise and background in raptors and upland birds; so rather naturally the Bighorn River Resort has become a supreme spot for good bird hunting and the ultimate "cast and blast."

Many of the resort's very knowledgeable and now multi-generational Crow guides—as capable of handling a brace of Brittanies as the oars on a float trip—got their professional start with the Forresters. The couple came to the Bighorn region in 1991 to manage/cook at hunting and fishing lodges and ended up in 1993 running Eagle's Nest Lodge before deciding to go out on their own in 1996.

Francine Forrester grew up in Wyoming. "I was a Forest Service brat, always backpacking, fishing, eating roasted marshmallows, and making cowboy coffee," Francine explained. Francine went to college, even was pre-med, but decided in 1982 to try cooking school instead. She attended Peter Kump's New York Cooking School in its first year when there were only six students and also worked in an Italian restaurant and then two resorts in the British West Indies—on the islands of Anguilla and St. Martin.

"I really learned about cooking there," Francine recalled. "Working in an open kitchen, meeting the lobster boats dockside, I literally lived and breathed food." Francine attracted sponsors to help her continue her culinary instruction through private tutors. And in 1985, Francine returned to her home state of Wyoming to a 20,000-acre, corporate retreat and guest ranch near Sheridan. There she met Nick, and they remained at Ucross Ranch—she as chef and he as manager—for five years.

"My favorite game bird to cook is pheasant," Francine said. "The breasts are large enough to experiment with and sauce, and the legs good for a nice confit. With pheasant, I also make a classic coq au vin using chanterelles and red wine."

Pear brandy, morels, plum, chokecherries, Calvados, demi-glace, sage, and, of course elk and grouse, are just some of the carefully chosen ingredients Francine cleverly strings together into her recipe designs. She confesses she doesn't go into the field herself anymore, only occasionally shooting skeet.

"I'd rather be in the kitchen," Francine said. "Whatever they bring me, I'll turn into something nice."

I believe Francine; and oh, how very nice for the guests at Bighorn River Resort that the kitchen is where she'd rather be.

Sautéed Pheasant Breast with Sage Rub and Roast Garlic Sauce

(SERVES 4)

1 garlic bulb

Olive oil

4 game bird breasts (any combination of pheasant, partridge, and grouse)

Sage Rub (see recipe below)

12 slices bacon

2 cups dark poultry stock or game bird stock

1/2 onion, chopped

1 apple, peeled, cored, and chopped

1 teaspoon cornstarch (optional)

1 tablespoon chokecherry syrup or maple syrup

1–2 teaspoons tamari

1 drop sesame oil

1 drop smoke essence

Salt

Preheat the oven to 350 degrees. Peel away the loose outer skin of the garlic and slice off the tips to expose the garlic. Place the garlic in a small baking pan and drizzle it with the olive oil. Roast the garlic in the oven for 45 minutes to 1 hour.

Bone the breasts by following the contour of the bone with a very sharp boning knife. Freeze the bones for later use or use them to make a quick stock. (Sauté the bones in water for a minute and then strain them to get a nice brown stock.) Lay the breasts on a sheet tray and remove the moisture with paper towels. Rub the Sage Rub (see recipe below) liberally over the prepared meat.

Heat a cast iron skillet and fry the bacon to accumulate 1/4 to 1/2 cup of fat. (Do not burn the bacon because the taste will transfer to the game meat. Duck fat is also very nice.) Remove the bacon when it is crisp and reserve it for another use. (Kitchen passersby usually solve this little dilemma.) Let the bacon fat cool slightly in the skillet, and then add the game meat and sauté it on both sides until browned but still rare.

Decrease the oven temperature to 325 degrees. Remove the meat to a sheet tray and bake it in the preheated oven to finish, approximately 10 minutes. (Do not overcook.)

Drain off all fat from the skillet. Deglaze the skillet with the stock. Add the onion and apple and the roasted garlic to taste to the skillet. (The garlic will squeeze easily out of its skin.) Cook in the liquid until soft.

Puree the mixture and if you prefer strain it through cheesecloth into a small saucepan. You may want to thicken the sauce with cornstarch dissolved in cold water. To the sauce add the chokecherry syrup or maple syrup, tamari, sesame oil, and smoke essence. Add salt to taste.

■ ■ ■

Sage Rub

1 tablespoon dry or chopped fresh sage
1/2 teaspoon sea salt
1/4 teaspoon white pepper
1/2–1 tablespoon sesame seed
1 teaspoon sugar

1/2 teaspoon garlic salt
1/2 teaspoon cardamom
Pinch of allspice
Pinch of cayenne

Combine all ingredients in a bowl.

This is excellent served over a ragout of wild mushrooms with a side of sweet squash or seasoned sweet potato cakes.

Game Bird Ravioli with Rosemary Garlic Oil

(SERVES 6 AS A FIRST COURSE
OR 4 AS A MAIN COURSE)

6 slices bacon

2 pheasant and 6 chukar and/or Hungarian partridge breasts, boned

2 shallots, minced

2 garlic cloves, minced

2 sprigs fresh rosemary, chopped

4 sun-dried tomatoes, finely chopped

Zest of 1 orange

1/4 cup sherry or vermouth

Salt

Cracked black pepper

1 cup ricotta cheese

Flour

1 package wonton wraps

2 egg whites, beaten

7 quarts water

4 tablespoons olive oil

Heat a large, cast iron skillet over medium-high heat. Cook the bacon until crisp, then remove, leaving the drippings. Cook the birds in the bacon drippings until medium rare. Remove the birds and finely chop them. Add the shallots, garlic, and rosemary to the bacon drippings and sauté until the shallots are tender, about 5 minutes. Return the birds to the pan, adding the sun-dried tomatoes, orange zest, and sherry or vermouth. Cook until the sherry or vermouth is reduced to 1 tablespoon, season with salt and pepper to taste, and remove to a bowl. (At this point, the filling can be covered tightly and refrigerated for 2 days.)

Just before you're ready to assemble the ravioli, add the ricotta cheese, mixing it in well.

Dust the work surface and a baking sheet lightly with flour. Lay 4 to 8 wonton wraps out individually on the work surface. Brush the entire surface of half of the wontons with the egg white. Center 1 tablespoon of the bird filling on the half of the wonton wraps that are brushed with egg, and cover the filling with the other half of the wonton wraps. Press around the edges to seal, making sure there are no creases or rips in the wonton because this will cause the filling to leak when cooked.

Trim the edges of the ravioli with a pasta cutter or a sharp knife into smaller squares or rounds. Discard the trimmings. Repeat until all of the wontons are used, placing them on the floured tray as you go. Cook immediately or cover tightly and refrigerate.

When ready to cook, bring the water to a boil in a pot and add the oil. Gently place the ravioli, no more than six or seven at a time, into the pot. Cook until the ravioli are transparent, about 2 minutes.

Remove the ravioli with a slotted spoon to a serving plate. Repeat the cooking process until all of the ravioli are cooked. Pour enough Rosemary Garlic Oil (see below) over the ravioli to season each one and serve.

■ ■ ■

Rosemary Garlic Oil

1 cup extra virgin olive oil
Several sprigs fresh rosemary
4 garlic cloves, minced

Heat the oil in a heavy saucepan over medium-high heat. (Do not over heat the oil, or it will taste burned and will burn the garlic and herbs when added.) When the oil is slightly hot, drop the rosemary and garlic into it and remove from the heat. Allow the rosemary to infuse the oil for at least 15 minutes, then remove the rosemary from the oil. The garlic should be browned. It is up to you whether to leave the garlic in or remove it. The garlic will be crunchy and adds a nice contrast to the soft ravioli.

Roast Breast of Pheasant with Essence of Sage

(SERVES 4)

1 tablespoon fresh or dry sage, crushed

2 tablespoons sugar

1 1/2 teaspoons white pepper

1 teaspoon salt

1 teaspoon fresh or dry thyme, crushed

1/2 teaspoon dried coriander

1/4 teaspoon cayenne

1/2 cup butter, clarified

4 pheasant breasts, boned and blotted dry with paper towels (reserve bones for Pheasant Stock)

1/2 cup cognac

2 tablespoons demi-glace (optional)

1 1/2 cups chicken stock or Pheasant Stock (see recipe below)

Preheat the oven to 350 degrees. In a bowl, mix the sage, sugar, pepper, salt, thyme, coriander, and cayenne. Blend the seasonings very well.

Heat half of the butter in a cast iron skillet gradually, being careful not to let the butter become too hot. When the skillet is hot, add the pheasant, tenderloin side down. Sprinkle the seasoning mix generously onto the pheasant and sauté until slightly browned. Turn pheasant and repeat.

Before it is fully cooked, while the meat is still rare under the tenderloin, remove the pheasant from the skillet to a baking pan large enough to hold the pheasant without stacking. Add the remaining butter to the skillet to brown additional breasts, if necessary. Remove and discard all excess butter from the skillet. Let the skillet cool slightly. Deglaze the skillet with the cognac, scraping the pan to loosen the meat and seasonings. Add the demi-glace, if using, and the chicken or Pheasant Stock (see recipe below). Reduce the sauce until it is thickened enough to coat 4 plates.

Place the partially cooked pheasant into the preheated oven. Bake for about 8 minutes. (Finishing the pheasant in the oven leaves the breasts much more tender than cooking completely in the skillet.)

Serve the pheasant on the sauced plates.

■ ■ ■

Pheasant Stock

Reserved pheasant bones
2 tablespoons butter
4 quarts water
1 onion, chopped
2 celery stalks, chopped
2 carrots, chopped
1 bay leaf
1 sprig thyme
6 black peppercorns

Place the bones in a pot large enough to hold at least 4 quarts of water. Add the butter to the pot and roast the bones on top of the stove until lightly browned. Add the water to cover, along with the onion, celery, carrots, bay leaf, thyme, and peppercorns. Boil for at least 2 hours and then strain.

Roast Prime Rib of Buffalo with Chokecherry Au Jus

1 boneless roast of buffalo prime rib*
2 cups hearty red wine
1/2 cup soy sauce
1 cup brewed dark coffee
6 garlic bulbs, roasted
2 tablespoons coarse sea salt
Cracked black pepper
1–2 cups brown stock
1/2 cup chokecherry syrup or jelly

Preheat the oven to 350 degrees. Place the roast in a roasting pan large enough to allow space around the meat. Pour the wine, soy sauce, and coffee over the roast.

Remove the skin of the garlic and crush the garlic into a paste. Spread the garlic evenly over the entire surface of the roast. Sprinkle the sea salt onto the roast and pepper to your taste. Place the roast in the preheated oven, basting occasionally until done to desired temperature. (Use a meat thermometer to test for temperature: 120 degrees will be rare, 135 medium rare, and above will be medium.) If the roasting pan becomes dry while cooking, add additional red wine and/or brown stock.

When finished, remove the roast and let it rest for 10 minutes. (The roast will continue to cook during this time so plan for this when testing for desired results.) During this resting period, move the roast to a cutting board, giving you access to the pan to make the au jus. Remove as much fat from the roasting pan as possible. Strain the remaining juice into a saucepan. Add the stock and the chokecherry syrup or jelly. Lightly cook until blended.

A third of a pound per person is a very adequate serving portion of this protein-rich meat. Cooking time is about 12 minutes per pound.

Chantale Gratton

Chef, Sevogle Salmon Club
Miramichi, New Brunswick, Canada

"Steve made me. There's no question about that!" Chantale Gratton stated emphatically. She was explaining how—and who—helped her attain exceptional chef-dom status, but in my mind the phrase flashed images of godfathers and "made" members of the Mafia. No, there's nothing as dramatic as that here, merely the pleasant reality of a young Canadian woman being encouraged and mentored in the ways of the culinary arts by her employer, although there is a kind of rise to power in this story.

When Steve Latner first bought the lease on the Sevogle Salmon Club, he interviewed several students at the local trade school where restaurant/catering skills were taught. Chantale was one of them. At the time, she could barely speak English; she'd come from a little town on the Acadian coast, Caraquet, where her mother and grandmother had run a wedding-catering business. Chantale worked her first summer at the camp in 1992. In the winter, Steve took her to Toronto to learn what it was to be a professional cook from Chef Mark McEwan of North 44 and Pronto restaurants. And Chantale learned well. She began to produce great meals and also to enjoy the challenge of creating, developing different taste sensations, and experimenting.

"I find cooking game to be very interesting, and I particularly like trying new ideas out on woodcock . . . and with partridge, too," Chantale confessed. "These days I've been using Asian recipes on fish and game."

Each year, Chantale and Steve plan the season's meals, inventing twenty new menus and importing many specialty items from Toronto for the 150 or so guests who will visit the club. But, of course, local ingredients continue to take center stage.

Ed and I first enjoyed Chantale's cooking when we were on our annual New Brunswick woodcock hunt. Steve, who is also a friend of ours, had invited our group to the club. This was back when our hunting group was still large, and the trip was ten days or so. We'd caravan through the province, sort of like gypsy hunters, our herd of jeeps loaded with dog kennels full of Brittanies, Llewellyn setters, or the guides' sterling pair of springers. Sandwiched around the dog boxes, we'd cram the other hunting paraphernalia of guns, ammo, topo maps, rain gear, waders—in case a duck-hunt opportunity presented itself—and more, always more. Morning till dark was spent in the woods. The nights were spent in motels where they didn't care if it was dogs, people, or both in the beds; plastic bathroom cups doubled as cocktail glasses; and there was no such thing as a nonsmoking room.

And the meals? As in the United States, New Brunswick food reflects its varying regional pockets of ethnic heritages. Menus definitely range: from overdone, unidentifiable meat accompanied by boiled white tubers, grey green beans, and Kool-Aid—usually the diet of the province's Anglo-interior—to the luscious French-based cuisine of the Acadian Peninsula with its mussels steamed in Pernod, fresh-from-the-ocean oysters, poached striped bass, and local wines that would rival their French cousins.

We reached the Sevogle Salmon Club mid-trip, coming off far too many days of eating fried or boiled food of questionable edibility. It had been raining for days, which meant the hunting had been scratchy. We brought with us lots of mud, wet clothes, and an attitude sorely in need of repair.

Winding through a long, balsam-lined dirt road, we came upon several cabins attached to the edge of a cliff overlooking the Sevogle River. Chantale had set the stage for an exquisite evening, scattering jack-o-lanterns carved with rising woodcock images around the light bulb–less camp. Flocks of candlelight timberdoodles flickered on the encircling evergreens and celebrated the October evening.

Steve handed us each a healthy shot of single-malt to warm our dampened bones. And while we took turns in the shower and dressed for dinner, Chantale served the hors d'oeuvres: smoked salmon from New Brunswick's Bay of Fundy coast and herbed toast-points carrying thin slices of woodcock breasts from local coverts, which were apparently more productive than the ones we'd visited lately.

Dinner started fashionably at ten with cold lobster salad and a corn and black bean soup; then came rack of lamb, a potato puree, and a magnificent vegetable dish of julienned zucchini and carrots plentifully blended with that most organically pungent and sensual of fungi—the white truffle. There were sorbets and imported ice creams accompanied by vanilla wafers—shaped by a cookie cutter to look like small salmon—cheeses and port, Cohibas, and glass upon glass of spectacular wines. My favorite that night was the ice wine from Ontario's Niagara region.

The meal was quintessential entertainment—bliss bordering on decadence—and Chantale's execution of the event had been perfect. More impressive, she'd managed it in a New Brunswick backwoods fishing and hunting camp.

On another visit, we were treated to appetizers of salted cod fritters, Malpec oysters on the half shell, and deep-fried wontons stuffed with cilantro-lime scallops. The first course was a lobster and leek bisque; then came a foie gras on toast and drizzled with balsamic vinegar; next a truffled risotto with grilled woodcock breasts. The main course was moose loin wrapped in pancetta, and the dessert included a chocolate bombe with a coulis of the tiny, wild strawberries *(fraises des bois)* and iced crème fraîche and mint. It was spectacular what local treats Chantale could find.

I wondered if Chantale's devotion to cooking with regional and wild foods wouldn't—as in my own case—inspire in her a desire to hunt. I knew she'd gotten her guide license and even become a warden. Surely the next step was to shoot her own ingredients.

As we arrived one fall in late afternoon, we spied the truck of the camp's head guide, Frenchy, backed into the entrance of a covert off the camp's access road. I chortled to myself, hopeful that Chantale was out shooting dinner with Frenchy. Instead we found Chantale at the camp. She laughed when I asked her why she wasn't out shooting.

"Oh, the guys are afraid of me with a gun," she said. "They think I already have too much power over them with the food."

Sevogle Grouse

(SERVES 4)

1/2 cup olive oil
1/3 cup truffle oil
1/4 cup champagne vinegar
1 tablespoon herbes de Provence
Salt
4 grouse breasts
Black pepper
4–6 slices pancetta, prosciutto, or Canadian bacon

In a large bowl, combine the olive oil, truffle oil, vinegar, herbes, salt, and pepper. Place the grouse in the marinade and marinate it at room temperature for at least 1 hour or up to 2 days in the refrigerator.

Remove the grouse from the marinade. Wrap each breast in a slice of pancetta, prosciutto, or Canadian bacon, securing with toothpicks.

Heat the grill. Place the grouse on the coolest side of the grill. Shut the lid and slow-cook for about 30 to 40 minutes, until the pancetta, prosciutto, or Canadian bacon is crispy.

Temmy's Salmon Croquettes

(SERVES 4)

2–3 shallots or scallions
Butter
2 cups fresh salmon, cooked and cut into small pieces
2 eggs
1 tablespoon chopped fresh dill
1 tablespoon fresh lemon juice
1 teaspoon honey mustard
1/2 teaspoon salt
1/2 teaspoon black pepper
1 red bell pepper, finely chopped
1 small potato, cooked and chopped
1/4–1/2 cup dried bread crumbs or matzo meal
Dill Mayonnaise (see recipe below)

In a skillet, sauté the shallots in a little butter until translucent.

In a bowl, combine the shallots, salmon, eggs, dill, lemon juice, honey mustard, salt, black pepper, bell pepper, potato, and bread crumbs and blend until smooth.

Form the mixture into small croquettes (burger-size patties). Chill the croquettes in the refrigerator for at least 30 minutes. In a large skillet, melt more butter and fry the croquettes over medium heat. Cook about 3 minutes each side until crispy. Serve with Dill Mayonnaise (see recipe below)

. . .

Dill Mayonnaise

1 cup mayonnaise

1/4 cup plain yogurt

4 green onions, chopped

1 tablespoon capers

1 tablespoon fresh dill, finely chopped

2 teaspoons Dijon mustard

2 teaspoons prepared white horseradish

1 tablespoon fresh lemon juice

In a bowl, combine all ingredients well.

Smoked Salmon

(SERVES 4)

1 quart water
1/4 cup salt
1 teaspoon soy sauce
1/4 cup brandy
2–4 grilse fillets, with skin

In a large bowl, combine the water, salt, soy sauce, and brandy to make a brine. Soak the fillets, skin side down, completely covered in the brine for several hours. Drain the fillets and place them, skin side down, on the rack at the far end of a drum-style barbecue. Build a charcoal fire in its attached firebox. Add fresh cut green fruitwood and smoke the fillets for 3 to 6 hours (depending on the thickness and number of fillets) at approximately 160 degrees. A chimney-vent controls the smoke and temperature.

Lobster with Chantale's Lobster Roe Sauce

(SERVES 4)

4 lobsters (1–1 1/2 pounds each)
Chantale's Lobster Roe Sauce (see recipe below)

In a large pot of boiling water, drop each lobster and cook for 10 minutes. Remove the lobsters and let cool slightly in the sink. Crack the claws to drain. Break off the tails and remove the roe for the sauce. Place each tail, body, and claws on plates and serve with Chantale's Lobster Roe Sauce for dipping (see recipe below).

■ ■ ■

Chantale's Lobster Roe Sauce

1/2 cup mayonnaise
1 tablespoon Dijon mustard
1/3 cup chopped chives
1 teaspoon tarragon
1/4 cup lobster roe (reserved from lobsters)
1 garlic clove, finely chopped
Splash white wine
Lemon juice

In a bowl, mix all the ingredients and lemon juice to taste. Refrigerate for at least 1 hour.

Smoked Oysters

(SERVES 4 AS HORS D'OEUVRE)

1/2 pound butter
Juice of 2 lemons
1 garlic clove, minced
1/4 teaspoon cayenne
2 dozen oysters

In a saucepan, melt the butter and mix it with the lemon juice, garlic, and cayenne. Let simmer together for a few minutes. Then turn off the heat, cover the saucepan and let the mixture steep for a while together.

Shuck the oysters and drizzle about half a teaspoon of the sauce into each shell.

Heat the grill. When the grill is ready, distribute the oysters on the grill and close the hood. Cook and smoke for 10 to 15 minutes. Serve immediately.

Michael Gray

Executive Chef, the Hanover Inn
Hanover, New Hampshire

"Don't leave the legs in the field." This was at least the third time Michael Gray—no relation to me, but executive chef at the Hanover Inn in New Hampshire—had offered this same advice in the space of an hour. Had it come from someone other than a hunter and a chef extremely well versed in game cooking, it could have been a remark open to misinterpretation and construed into something quite bizarre. Whose legs aren't being left in the field? Bird legs!

Michael knows that many hunters consider the legs of woodcock, partridge, pheasant—all the tough-legged birds—inedible, extraneous parts that should be left alongside the entrails in the field dressing of game birds. The mere thought seems to be cause for his increasingly adamant mandate.

"Yes, save the legs, marinate and then braise them using a lot of fat, as in a *confit*," Michael rattled off in hyper-chef mode. "Now remove the legs, reserve the braising liquid, and grind up the braised leg meat. Pound the breasts and then stuff them, like a forced meat, with the ground leg meat, and then poach the breasts. What flavor! You always get more flavor from meat cooked on the bone—the *leg* bone."

I get it. Save the legs. But just how did Michael come to get it?

Michael grew up in northern Rhode Island and was taught to shoot at a nearby shooting range by neighbor friends. Pheasants populated the cornfields of Butterfly Farms on the backside of his local golf course and provided Michael with his first hunt. Michael admits he never was actually taught to hunt and relied primarily on trial and error to get birds. But Michael liked being out there and by high school had thought he would major in forestry in college and work for the National Park Service. Then a guidance counselor, or, Michael tries to recall, maybe it was his dad, suggested he look at the new culinary school at Johnson & Wales University.

Michael enjoyed cooking and had worked as a short-order cook at a pizza parlor. He'd also cooked at the golf club dining room, moving from dishwasher to head cook in an instant promotion when the chef failed to show up for work. It proved fortuitous for Michael, leading him to professional culinary training at Johnson & Wales, working summers at restaurants on Cape Cod.

After college, Michael left New England to take a position as sous-chef at Caneel Bay Plantation in St. John. Caneel Bay was at the time a Rockresort—a chain of hotels owned by Laurence Rockefeller—so when the opportunity presented itself it was a natural for Michael to return to New England and another Rockresort, the Woodstock Inn in Vermont. Michael stayed three years before heading to Boston where he was sous-chef to the well-known Lydia Shire, when she was executive chef at the Bostonian Hotel. Michael next moved to Cambridge and the restaurant Rarity at the Charles Hotel.

Then he heard from the chef at the Woodstock Inn about an executive chef opening at the Hanover Inn in New Hampshire. In 1985, Michael became the Inn's youngest executive chef, a big job considering the Dartmouth College–owned inn required not only culinary management of the elegant dining room and a significant catering business but also the development of a second, bistro-style restaurant.

"Sometimes we cater dinner for six at the president's house, a banquet for 400 at the gymnasium, a class reunion cocktail party in one of our function rooms or Alumni Hall, and have the two Inn restaurants filled to capacity, too," Michael said matter-of-factly.

In addition, when Michael arrived, he was given a culinary mandate to create "an aggressive food program with upgrades to both outside and in-house menus."

The new menus would showcase New England foods. Of course, this meant seafood—striped bass, salmon, mussels, and clams—and cranberries and maple syrup. But for Michael it also meant venison, rabbit, pheasant, and duck. His own hunting and consequently wild game preparation had been curtailed with his wife and daughter's pronouncement of "no fur or feathers" in the home kitchen. And, of course, a commercial operation could not buy wild game. But Michael made certain he bought from purveyors who sold local farm-raised game satisfying both the new menu requirements and his own desire to work with game.

"The flavor of the meat is reflected in what the animal has been eating," Michael said. "Wild game is certainly more flavorful and has a different texture than pen-raised, but at least if you buy locally raised game, it's been eating what the wild ones eat."

Michael believes European partridge are the closest in flavor of all restaurant birds to tasting wild. But certainly the superior flavor of Michael's game dishes can primarily be attributed to his imaginative cooking techniques—and, of course, to his use of the legs.

Michael is certainly not alone in his exaltation of game bird legs. Two of my hunting friends—enamored so completely with an appetizer of sautéed woodcock legs—once risked possible prison time while attempting to bring back a bag full of the little legs collected during our week-long New Brunswick hunt. The customs agents were not happy about migratory bird parts coming into the United States without the body and its obligatory one wing—not to mention in a quantity that appeared to far exceed the limit for just two hunters. We'd been a party of eight, and they now had all the legs. Clearly they had not thought this through, although I'd done nothing to discourage the plan. Quite the contrary. I was really disappointed when the legs were confiscated.

Then as Michael said for the fourth time, "Don't leave the legs in the field." I envisioned my leg-loving friends as they passed over their woodcock cache to the authorities. I wondered if Michael Gray would have done the same. Or would he have done like this Gray (me, I mean!) might have considered: risked freedom, tried to dazzle the patrolmen with an eloquent explanation of the culinary necessity of bird legs, and absconded with them into Maine? Well, he may be Michael Gray-no-relation, but when it comes to bird legs, I believe I've met my soul mate.

Herb-Cured Duck Breast with Cranberry and Tawny Port Sauce

(SERVES 4)

1 large duck or Canada goose, breast and legs removed and carcass
    bones reserved for roasting and stock
Marinade (see recipe below)
Salt
Pepper
Maple syrup
1/2 cup white wine
1 carrot, sliced
1 onion, sliced
1 celery stalk, sliced
1 teaspoon herbes de Provence
2 tablespoons unsalted butter
3 tablespoons olive oil
Tawny Port Sauce (see recipe below)

Preheat the oven to 350 degrees. Marinate the breasts and legs overnight in the Marinade (see recipe below). Rub the legs with salt and pepper and them drizzle with maple syrup. Place the carcass in a roasting pan. Reserve the breasts for cooking. Place the legs on the carcass (like a saddle on a horse), prick them with a fork, and roast them in the preheated oven for an hour, or until juice runs clear. Baste with drippings and any extra marinade.

Remove the legs and bones and hold at room temperature. Deglaze the roasting pan with the wine and return the carcass to the pan. Add water almost to cover.

In a skillet, sauté the carrot, onion, and celery along with the herbes in 1 tablespoon of the butter until soft, making a mirepoix. Add the mirepoix to the bones in the roasting pan. Continue to roast for 1 to 2 hours to make au jus or stock.

Prepare the Tawny Port Sauce (see recipe below).

To finish the dish, heat a large skillet or frying pan, score the breast skin and sauté the breast meat in the olive oil. When breast gets crisp, turn. Cook 3 to 4 minutes on moderate heat, or less if you prefer rare. The legs can be warmed in a high oven, or you may also sear them in the skillet to crisp them while you let the breasts rest 5 minutes.

Place the legs on a warmed plate. Sauce the plate and slice the breast the long way and fan. Garnish the plate with cooked cranberries from the Tawny Port Sauce.

Serve with buttered parsnips or a combination of root vegetables.

. . .

Marinade

6 crushed juniper berries
1 cup crushed cranberries
2 shallots, finely chopped
3 sprigs fresh thyme
1/4 cup port
1/4 teaspoon cracked black pepper

In a large bowl, combine the juniper berries, cranberries, shallots, thyme, port, and pepper.

Tawny Port Sauce

3–4 dozen cranberries
2 cups tawny port
2 cups stock or au jus
2 tablespoons maple syrup
Remaining Marinade
Salt
Pepper
1 tablespoon butter

In a saucepan, combine the cranberries and port. Reduce them to half. Add the stock or au jus, remaining marinade and syrup and reduce to half. Adjust seasonings and sweetness/tartness to desired flavor. Add salt and pepper to taste. Whisk in the butter to thicken the sauce slightly.

Tom's Camp Lake Trout

(SERVES 4)

1 whole laker (3–4 pounds), cleaned

1/2 stick butter, sliced

Salt

2 teaspoons cracked black pepper

Herbs of choice (I prefer thyme and tarragon)

3–4 lemon slices

4 or 5 celery leaf tops or hearts or 5 celery seeds

1 small onion, sliced

1/8 cup olive oil or peanut oil (optional)

1/4 cup soy sauce

1/4 cup wine or cider vinegar

2 garlic cloves, crushed

1–2 tablespoons sugar or maple syrup

Open the laker cavity and make 3 or 4 cuts along the backbone from inside of the belly, each about 1 1/2 inches long, to allow the flavors to get to the thick parts of fish. Push the butter into the slits and sprinkle salt, pepper, and the herbs in the cavity. Add the lemon, celery, and onion to the cavity. If the fish is thick, slice the outside of the fish also, 1 or 2 times, between the gill plate and dorsal fin, about halfway through the fish.

Place the fish on a double layer of foil. Sprinkle it with salt and pepper. Add the oil, if using, and the remaining butter, and the soy sauce, vinegar, maple syrup, and garlic. Wrap up the laker and let it set for 30 to 45 minutes, shaking it once in a while.

Preheat the oven to 350 degrees or heat the grill. Bake or grill the laker for 10 to 15 minutes per side. Open the foil and test the laker with a blunt toothpick (break tip off pick) at the thickest area of the fish. A very slight resistance of the fish will indicate doneness. Let the fish rest for 5 to 10 minutes, slide onto a platter, and dig in!

Scampi-Style Striper

(SERVES 4)

4–5 small striper fillets, skin on, scored

Salt

Pepper

Wondra flour*

Olive oil

1 teaspoon finely chopped shallots

2 tablespoons butter

1 teaspoon garlic

1/4 cup white wine

Lemon wedge

Worcestershire sauce

2 tablespoons finely chopped Italian parsley

1 teaspoon fresh chervil

Sprinkle both sides of the fish with salt and pepper then dredge it in flour.

In a large skillet, heat the oil to light smoke and sear the fillets skin side down, turning when they are medium brown and cooking for 2 minutes per side.

Remove the fillets to a warm platter, pour off the oil, and return the skillet to the stove. Add the butter, shallots, and garlic and sauté until soft. Deglaze the skillet with the wine and dribble the mixture over the fillets. Add the lemon wedge and a dash of Worcestershire sauce and finish with the parsley and chervil.

*Wondra is a great flour for thickening and for flouring an item for sautéing.

Striper Crab

(SERVES 4)

2 quarts water
2 onions
4 stalks celery
2–3 tablespoons Old Bay Seasoning
Salt
1 striper fillet (2–3 pounds), skinned and boned
2 lemons

In a pot, bring the water to a boil and cook the onions and celery. Add the Old Bay Seasoning then add salt to taste. As the mixture continues to boil, drop in the fish. Remove the pot from the heat and set it uncovered on the side of the stove, until it is cool enough to handle.

As the poaching liquid cools, it gently cooks the fish to a perfect doneness. (This works great with salmon, without the Old Bay Seasoning.) The fish stays moist and at room temperature. It is perfect for a cold salad or entrée.

Once the fish is cool or cold, flake it with a fork. Now it looks and tastes like crabmeat. Serve with lemon wedges. (I made crab cakes with this, and most people could not tell the difference. It's great for those who love crab but can't eat it.)

My Favorite Duck Marinade
(SERVES 4)

This berry-flavored marinade is great for a 3 to 5 pound venison roast, pot roast, stew, or steak.

2 teaspoons cracked black pepper
3 sprigs thyme
2 tablespoons juniper berries, crushed
1 1/2 cups chopped cranberries, fresh or frozen
6 shallots, quartered
1 cup port
1/2 cup maple syrup, grade B preferred, or C

Rub the meat with the pepper and thyme. Sprinkle the juniper berries, cranberries, and shallots on top. Pour the port and syrup over the meat. Depending on the thickness of the meat, marinate for 24 to 48 hours.

Tailgate Partridge

(SERVES 6)

1 1/2 tablespoons cracked black pepper

1/2 tablespoon juniper berries, crushed

3 sprigs thyme, chopped

1 sprig rosemary, chopped

3 garlic cloves, chopped

1 orange, juice and zest

1/2 lemon, juice and zest

1 bottle burgundy or Merlot red wine

6 partridges, split and quartered

Salt

Pepper

Olive oil

6–8 plum tomatoes, peeled, seeded, and quartered

8 whole peeled shallots

6–8 large portobello mushrooms, cleaned and grilled

In a large bowl, combine the pepper, juniper, thyme, rosemary, and garlic. Add the orange juice and zest and lemon juice and zest along with 2 cups of the wine. Marinate the legs and breasts in this mixture overnight.

Sprinkle the legs and breasts with salt and pepper. Heat the oil in a skillet and sear the legs and breasts. Set the breasts aside.

Place the legs in a casserole or braiser along with the marinade, tomatoes, and shallots. Simmer, covered, for 30 to 45 minutes. Add the breasts to the casserole, adjust the salt and pepper, and add the remaining wine. Simmer for 1/2 hour. Add the mushrooms and simmer for another 15 to 30 minutes or let cool and reheat the next day. (Anything braised or stewed is better the next day.)

Serve the partridge on crushed boiled potatoes or potato gnocchi.

Chowda Sauce for Striper

(SERVES 4)

2 tablespoons salt pork
4 tablespoons onion, shallot, or leek, chopped into 1/8-inch cubes
2 tablespoons celery or celery root, chopped into 1/8-inch cubes
Pinch fresh thyme
1 bay leaf
1/4 cup fish stock or water
1/2–1 cup chopped potato (Yukon preferred)
1 cup cream
Salt
Pepper

In a skillet, cook the salt pork until crisp. Add the onion, shallot, or leek and the celery or celery root and cook lightly. Add the thyme and bay leaf. Deglaze the skillet with the stock or water and add the potato. Simmer, reduce, and then add the cream and reduce again until it is the desired consistency. Add salt and pepper to taste.

Use this sauce on baked, grilled, or sautéed striper.

Chris Hastings

Executive Chef and Co-owner,
the Hot and Hot Fish Club restaurant
Birmingham, Alabama

I once spent a week in the woods with my own high priests and celebrity chefs, hunting woodcock and eating my way into a kind of fish and game state of culinary and gastronomic euphoria. Wayne Nish (see p. 171) and Chantale Gratton (see p. 38)—two of the hunt's chef participants—who I'd previously hunted and/or cooked with—were along again. And my friend and hunting companion Charles Gaines—clearly in a move to induce utter decadence—this time also invited Chris Hastings, an exquisite chef from Birmingham, Alabama, to accompany us on the hunt. Indeed, the Hastings group knew how to celebrate the ritual of eating.

Such depth of food spirituality was clearly seeded early in Chris.

"It seems like my most fond memories revolve around cooking in the kitchen with my mother or sneaking away to off-the-wall, funky fun restaurants she knew about," Chris recalled.

Chris grew up in Charlotte, North Carolina, but he spent summers on Pawleys Island, South Carolina, where his great-great-grandfather, Hugh Fraser, had emigrated from Scotland in the early 1800s and become a rice planter. Like many Southern gentlemen, Fraser was a member of the Pawleys Hot and Hot Fish Club, "for men who loved food and loved to fish." There on the island, Chris became the designated "creek boy," always digging clams, trapping crabs, collecting oysters, fishing, and then, of course, cooking and eating family-style around a big table. (Now the Hot and Hot Fish Club name—along with a harvest table that can seat fourteen people—are signature features of Chris's Birmingham restaurant.)

Chris's professional culinary career started, like that of many chefs, when he was in high school, busing and dishwashing at a local restaurant. But when he was eighteen, Chris decided—perhaps in response to his mother's death—to attend Johnson & Wales Culinary School in Providence, Rhode Island. Chris graduated from their two-year program, and in 1984, he moved to sous-chef at the Ritz-Carlton in Atlanta. From there, Chris moved to Birmingham and first became sous-chef at Highlands Bar and Grill and then spearheaded the opening of the sister restaurant Bottega. In 1987, Chris and his new wife, Idie, moved to San Francisco where she attended culinary school and Chris helped open the Lark Creek Inn with Bradley Ogden.

Although Chris attributes his strong work ethic—the willingness to commit and understand that you have a job to do—to the French and Austrian chefs he worked under at the Ritz, he believes that Ogden most influenced his culinary style.

"Brad's unrelenting pursuit of intense, clear flavor was never compromised," Chris said. "He also opened my eyes to the local farmer and how he could impact the food and help set it apart from the others—searching out the very best—always looking for the peak of seasonal ripeness."

Ah yes, seasonality, that cornerstone of game cooking.

In 1995, with the birth of their first son and a belief that the South was a better place to raise children than San Francisco, the Hastings returned to Birmingham where they opened the Hot and Hot Fish Club.

"In the South, and very much in Birmingham, there is a deeply entrenched hunting and fishing culture," Chris said. "It is taken very, very seriously."

Chris is a self-taught hunter, spending camping trips as a boy with his non-hunting father first shooting squirrels, and then later dove. Today Chris is a passionate wing shooter, preferring the very wildest of the game birds—turkey grouse, woodcock, and duck—not only in the field but in the kitchen as well. Of course, Chris is prohibited from serving wild game in his restaurant, but the farm-raised game birds segue well into his menu's seasonality—even in the non-hunting season of summer. Chris offers smoked and grilled quail with summer vegetables and black pepper dressing as an appetizer to an entrée of July's wild mushrooms—morels and chanterelles—pasta or wild king salmon paillard with avocado, tomato, red onion, and lime vinaigrette.

But Chris admits that the most interesting and challenging aspects of cooking game birds can only come from the wild ones.

"I've become a perfect butcher, knowing how to clean the bird, what to do with the 'awfuls,' and utilizing the whole bird," Chris said, as an experienced hunter-chef. "I'm not throwing anything in the garbage. And this demands using a lot of different culinary processes—from making sausage to a *confit* of those tough legs—I love that."

Chris makes this comment to me at the conclusion of our wonderful New Brunswick dinner—the one where the cacophony of chef talent has culminated into a gastronomic orgy. I'm reeling. Is it the wine, the incredible food, the great day in the field? It's all of these, of course, but it's also that I'm getting a peek at the soul of a great chef—a great game chef.

Wild Turkey, Watercress, Tomato, Avocado, and Goat Cheese Salad

(SERVES 4)

1 tablespoon Dijon mustard

4 tablespoons buttermilk

Dash of salt

Dash of pepper

8 thinly sliced medallions wild
    turkey breast

2 cups fresh bread crumbs

4 ounces peanut oil

2 heads watercress, stemmed

12 cherry tomatoes, sliced

1 avocado, stemmed

Lemon juice

4 ounces Dijon vinaigrette (see
    recipe below)

4 ounces goat cheese

In a large bowl, combine the mustard, buttermilk, salt, and pepper. Marinate the turkey in the mixture for 1 hour. Dredge the marinated turkey in the bread crumbs. Place the turkey on parchment paper on a plate. (It can be held for up to 2 hours in the refrigerator.)

Just prior to serving, in a cast iron skillet, heat the oil until smoking. Add the breaded turkey. Brown each side for approximately 2 minutes. Remove from the heat and keep warm.

In a small bowl, combine the watercress, tomatoes, and avocado with a little squeeze of lemon juice to prevent discoloration.

Toss the avocado mixture in Dijon Vinaigrette (see recipe below). Place a layer of salad on a plate and place 1 slice turkey on top. Place another layer of salad followed by another turkey slice. Top with the remaining salad. Crumble goat cheese over the top and serve immediately.

■ ■ ■

Dijon Vinaigrette

1 tablespoon Dijon mustard
Juice of 1 lemon
3 ounces olive oil
Salt
Pepper
Fresh thyme or chives

In a bowl, combine all ingredients and reserve.

Whole Roasted Woodcock with Fall Vegetable Gratin and Porcini Mushroom Giblet Gravy

(SERVES 4)

8 head-on woodcock, skin on too if possible

Salt

Pepper

24 sage leaves

8 slices pork fat back (4- by 4-inches and extremely thin)

2 ounces chopped bacon

1/2 cup butter

3 tablespoons chopped shallots

8 woodcock livers, sliced

8 woodcock hearts, sliced

4 intestinal tracts (optional)

10 ounces porcini mushrooms

1/2 cup Madeira

1 cup chicken stock

1 tablespoon chopped parsley

1 tablespoon finely sliced chives

1 tablespoon fresh chopped thyme

Fall Vegetables Gratin (see recipe below)

Preheat the oven to 500 degrees. Season the cavities of the woodcock with salt, pepper, and two sage leaves. Tuck the head of the woodcock back and into the base of the wing. Season the outside of the woodcock with salt and pepper and lay a sage leaf on the breast. Tightly wrap 1 pork fat slice over each woodcock, overlapping on the backbone. Secure with a piece of kitchen string.

Place the woodcock in a heavy-bottom, ovenproof sauté pan. Roast the woodcock in the preheated oven for 25 minutes. Remove and keep warm.

To make the Porcini Mushroom Giblet, in the same skillet, cook the bacon until crispy. Add 1/4 cup of the butter and the shallots, livers, hearts, and intestines, if using, and cook for 2 minutes over medium-high heat. Add the mushrooms and cook for an additional 3 minutes. Add the Madeira and cook for an additional 3 minutes. Add the chicken stock and cook down by half. Stir in the parsley, chives, thyme, and the remaining butter. Remove from the heat.

To serve, place a piece of warm Fall Vegetable Gratin (see recipe below) on center of each plate. Place 2 woodcock on top of the gratin on each plate. Spoon porcini gravy over each woodcock and serve immediately.

• • •

Fall Vegetable Gratin

Butter (for pan)
2 parsnips, peeled and cut into 1/16-inch thick slices
2 potatoes, peeled and cut into 1/16-inch thick slices
2 turnips, peeled and cut into 1/16-inch thick slices
1 rutabaga, peeled and cut into 1/16-inch thick slices
1/3 cup butter
Salt
Pepper
1 teaspoon fresh thyme
2/3 cup heavy cream

Preheat the oven to 350 degrees. Butter a small 6- by 6-inch ovenproof baking dish. Layer the parsnips, potatoes, turnips, and rutabagas in the pan. Season with the 1/3 cup butter and the salt, pepper, and thyme as you layer. Pour the cream over all. Cover and bake in the preheated oven for 30 minutes. Uncover and cook for an additional 15 minutes. Remove and keep warm until ready to serve.

Seared Black Grouper with Purple Mashed Potatoes, Steamed Asparagus, and Crawfish Remoulade

(SERVES 4)

Aioli is homemade garlic-flavored mayonnaise. For a quick version, mix 1/2 cup mayonnaise with 2 to 4 crushed cloves garlic or to taste.

Purple Potatoes (see recipe below)

Crawfish Remoulade (see recipe below)

4 portions black grouper (5 ounces each)

Salt

Freshly ground black pepper

1/4 cup peanut oil

12 spears jumbo asparagus, peeled and blanched

2 tablespoons unsalted butter, melted, or olive oil

Prepare the Purple Potatoes (see recipe below) and Crawfish Remoulade (see recipe below).

Preheat the oven to 400 degrees. Season the grouper with salt and pepper.

Wrap the handles of a heavy, ovenproof skillet completely with aluminum foil. Heat the oil in the skillet over medium-high heat. Add the grouper and brown quickly on each side. Transfer the skillet to the preheated oven and bake 4 to 5 minutes or until the grouper is just opaque.

In another skillet, sauté the asparagus in the butter or olive oil just until tender. Season with salt and pepper.

Spoon mashed potatoes on each of 4 serving plates and arrange the fish on the potatoes. Lean 3 asparagus spears on each piece of fish. Top evenly with Crawfish Remoulade.

• • •

Crawfish Remoulade

4 ounces fresh crawfish tail meat
1/2 cup aioli
4 scallions, minced
1 roasted red bell pepper finely
   chopped

Juice of 1 lemon
Salt
Freshly ground black pepper
Cayenne

In a bowl, mix the crawfish, aioli, scallions, bell pepper, lemon juice, and salt, black pepper, and cayenne to taste. Cover and set aside.

• • •

Purple Potatoes

8 small purple potatoes, peeled
   and sliced
Salt

1/4 cup unsalted butter
1/2 cup heavy cream
Freshly ground black pepper

Place the potatoes in a medium saucepan and cover with salted water. Bring to a boil. Reduce the heat and simmer just until tender. Drain and pat the potatoes dry with paper towels. In the saucepan, cook the butter and cream over medium heat until the butter melts and the mixture simmers. Add the potatoes and salt and pepper to taste and mash. Cover and keep warm in warming oven or on top of the hot stove.

Southern Bouillabaisse

(SERVES 2)

6 Florida hoppers (or other large shrimp), with heads on

1/4 pound Appalachia Bay scallops

6 Charleston littlenecks

6 mussels

1/4 pound black grouper

2 large stone crab claws

2 oranges, 1 for zesting

1 small leek

3 small carrots, peeled

2 stalks celery

5 Roma tomatoes

3 large garlic cloves

1 bulb fennel, with tops

6 sprigs thyme

1 bay leaf

1 large bunch basil

1/2 cup vegetable stock (optional)

1 lemon

2 large shallots

1 bunch Italian parsley

2 tablespoons butter

4 tablespoons virgin olive oil

1 teaspoon Spanish saffron, ground and toasted

Salt

Pepper

Peel the shrimp of all shell except the heads and tails. Set aside. Reserve the shells. Pick the feet off the bay scallops and set aside. Combine the feet with the shells. Wash the clams and mussels. Cut the grouper into 4 1-ounce pieces and set aside. Crack the stone crab claws with the back of a knife and set aside.

In a large stainless steel saucepan, combine the shrimp shells and scallop feet, orange zest, 1/3 of the leek, 1 carrot, 1 stalk celery, 2 Roma tomatoes crushed, 1 clove garlic, fennel trimmings, thyme, bay leaf, basil stems, and stock. Bring to a boil, reduce to a simmer, and cook for 40 minutes. Strain. Hold in the refrigerator.

Blanch, peel, seed, and quarter the remaining Roma tomatoes. Reserve. With a very sharp peeler, peel 3 orange peel strips from the orange, without any bitter white pith. Do the same for the lemon. Take the fennel bulb that been trimmed of its outer two layers and put into the broth and cut it in half. Remove the core. Turn it on its side and cut it into thin strips. Reserve. Split the remaining two-thirds of the leek in half with the root attached. Place the flat side on a cutting board and cut it into 1/2-inch thick half moons. Reserve. Cut the remaining carrots into thin round slices. Reserve. Peel the remaining celery stalk of its strings and cut into thin moon shaped pieces about 1/4-inch thick. Finely chop the remaining garlic clove. Peel and chop the shallot. Reserve. Wash and pick flat leaf parsley, chop coarsely and reserve. Pick basil and fennel and thyme, reserve for last minute chopping.

In a large heavy-bottomed stainless steel saucepan, heat 1 tablespoon of the butter and 1/4 cup of the olive oil. Add the shallots and garlic cooking over medium-high heat for 2 minutes, stirring constantly and not allowing to brown at all. If it is too high, lower the heat. Add the fennel, carrots, celery, leek, saffron, orange zest, and lemon zest. Cook for 3 or 4 minutes until tender. Add the clams and mussels and reserved tomatoes. Cook for about 2 more minutes. Add the seafood broth and turn up to high heat. Cover. Cook for 1 more minute. Add the shrimp, grouper, and stone crab claws, cover and cook for 1 more minute. Remove lid and add the remaining butter and olive oil, chopped fennel, basil, parsley, salt, and pepper. Carefully mix in and remove from heat.

Arrange the seafood attractively in a bowl with the vegetables and pour broth three-quarters up the bowl.

Note: This dish is terrific served with just-grilled sourdough croutons on the edge of the bowl and drizzled with rouille. A nice addition to this dish is half of a fried soft shell crab placed on last, carefully nestled among the other seafood.

Sautéed Breast of Grouse with Roasted Winter Vegetables and Thyme Dijon Sauce

(SERVES 4)

4 boneless grouse breasts

Black pepper

1 tablespoon chopped fresh thyme

Salt

12 strips pancetta, thinly sliced

2 ounces peanut oil

6 ounces butter

2 shallots, chopped

1 large parsnip, peeled and roasted

3 baby carrots, peeled and blanched

4 cipollini onions, peeled and roasted

4 baby turnips, blanched

4 baby beets, peeled and blanched

2 cups Grouse Stock (see recipe below)

1 tablespoon Dijon mustard

1/2 cup heavy cream

2 tablespoons chopped fresh parsley

Take the grouse and crack black pepper on both sides. Sprinkle a little thyme on the grouse and add a little salt. Lay the pancetta side by side, slightly overlapping the strips. Lay the grouse on the pancetta, wrapping the two ends together on the tenderloin side of the breast. Hold in the refrigerator until ready to cook.

Preheat the oven to 400 degrees. In a large cast iron skillet or heavy-bottomed ovenproof sauté pan, heat the oil. Once smoking hot, add the grouse, seamless side down, in the pan. Cook until golden brown. Flip over and cook the same. Remove the grouse from the skillet. Hold on a warm plate.

Pour out the excess oil from the skillet and add 2 tablespoons of the butter. Add the shallots and the remaining thyme. Add the parsnip, carrots, onions, turnips, and beets. Sauté for 3 to 4 minutes over medium high heat, not browning the vegetables.

In a separate pan, combine the Game Stock (see recipe below) and mustard. Reduce down to 3/4 cup. Add the cream and reduce to 1 cup.

Place the breasts on top of the vegetables in the skillet and place in oven for 5 minutes. (Do not overcook. Remember the breasts are already 60 percent cooked from the browning.) Once the grouse is in the oven, heat the sauce to a simmer. Whisk in the remaining butter and add the parsley. Turn off the heat and keep warm.

Arrange the vegetables around each plate. Put 1 breast per person on the vegetables and spoon over approximately 2 ounces of sauce per person. Serve immediately.

■ ■ ■

Grouse Stock

Grouse legs and bones   1 carrot
2 cups mirepoix   1 celery stick
1 onion   Sprigs thyme

After boning out the breast, rinse the carcass in cold water. If you do not want to use the legs in the dish, include them in the stock. Coarsely chop the bones and put into a stockpot. Cover the bones with water. Bring to a simmer. Skim off the foam and excess fat. Add the mirepoix and equal parts of onion, carrots, and celery. Add a few sprigs of fresh thyme and simmer for 1 1/2 hours. Strain. (At this point, you can freeze any excess stock. It will hold only for a few days in the refrigerator.)

Grilled Breast of Teal with Hunter-Style Risotto

(SERVES 4)

1 teaspoon cracked black pepper
1 teaspoon ground juniper
1 teaspoon chopped fresh thyme
2 cloves garlic, crushed
4 tablespoons olive oil
8 teal breasts

Par Cooked Risotto (see recipe below)
Hunter-Style Risotto (see recipe below)
Truffle oil
16 fried whole sage leaves (for garnish)

In a bowl, combine the pepper, juniper, thyme, garlic, and oil. Marinate the teal in this mixture for 24 hours, covered in the refrigerator.

Prepare the Par Cooked Risotto (see recipe below).

One hour before ready to serve, fire up the grill. When the coals become white, grill the teal until rare to medium rare. Keep them in a warm place until ready to serve. Begin cooking the Hunter-Style Risotto (see recipe below).

Divide the Hunter Style Risotto into four serving bowls. Slice the grilled teal into thin slices cut on a bias. Place the teal on top of the risotto. Drizzle with the truffle oil, garnish with fried whole sage leaves, and serve immediately.

• • •

Par Cooked Risotto

2 tablespoons peanut oil
4 ounces arborio rice
6 ounces white wine
2 bay leaves

4 sprigs fresh thyme
10 ounces chicken stock
1 small white onion, finely chopped
1 large leek, finely chopped

In a saucepan, heat the peanut oil to medium-high heat. Add the onion, leek and then the rice. Coat the rice in oil. Add the wine, bay leaves, and thyme. Reduce the heat to low. Stir the rice until the liquid is reduced by half. Add about a quarter of the stock and continue to stir. Continue process of adding stock and cooking until all of the stock is incorporated. (The risotto will be cooked three-quarters of the way at this point.)

Spread the risotto on a sheet pan to cool. Refrigerate until ready to use.

■ ■ ■

Hunter-Style Risotto

2 tablespoons chopped bacon, finely chopped

1 tablespoon chopped shallot

1/2 tablespoon chopped garlic

8 ounces chopped chanterelle mushrooms

1/4 cup chopped carrots

1/4 cup chopped celery

1/4 cup chopped onions

1/4 cup chopped leeks

1 teaspoon chopped fresh thyme

2 tablespoons chicken or duck livers

1/2 cup duck sausage, chopped or good quality Italian sausage

1 tablespoon paprika

8 ounces Par Cooked Risotto (see recipe above)

8 ounces chicken stock

2 tablespoons butter

2 tablespoons chopped fresh flat leaf parsley

1 teaspoon chopped chives

Salt

Pepper

In a skillet, cook the bacon until crisp. Add the shallot, garlic, mushrooms, carrots, celery, onions, leeks, and thyme. Sauté over medium heat until tender. Add the livers and sausage and cook for 1 minute. Add the risotto. Stir over low heat and add 4 ounces of the stock. Stir and allow the rice to slowly absorb the stock. Add the remaining stock and continue to stir. Add the butter, parsley, and chives. Season to taste with paprika, salt and pepper.

Michel and Cynthia Keller

Co-owners and Chefs, Restaurant du Village
Chester, Connecticut

"Michel and I began to celebrate Festival Diana, Goddess of the Hunt, at our Restaurant du Village the first fall we owned the restaurant," Cynthia Keller reminisced. "Ever since then, we annually pay homage to Diana the Huntress, the land, and the animals of our hunt."

The husband-and-wife chef team of Michel and Cynthia Keller began when they purchased the established Chester, Connecticut, restaurant in 1990. The partnership combined their distinct but complementary culinary styles, retained the wonderful French cuisine of the restaurant, and brought dimension and personality to classically based European dishes—which also prompted an increase in the amount of game on the menu.

I had the pleasure of first sampling their cooking not at the restaurant but at the home of Chet and Penny Reneson, where the bounty of all of our hunting seasons was parlayed into a huge game dinner. Of course, several guests brought contributions, and Michel acted as part supplier and—along with Cynthia—part preparer.

Michel grew up in the Alsace region of France, the son and grandson of pastry chefs. As a child, Michel accompanied his father on hunting excursions, mostly for rabbits, hares, roebuck deer, and boar. Michel once watched his father break the barrel of a shotgun over a charging boar. He learned not only to hunt from his father but trained under him as a pastry chef. When

Michel turned fourteen, he began his professional apprenticeship at Kohler Rhem pastry shop in Colmar, Alsace.

Michel moved to the United States in 1962 and assisted former White House pastry chef Albert Cumin and master chef Pierre Franey in consulting to Howard Johnson restaurants. Michel spent two years in the U.S. military as a mess sergeant at Fort Sills, Oklahoma, and then moved to New York City to bake at the Elysee Pastry Shop. In 1983, he developed the pastry menu for the new restaurant Prunelle.

"I was living in Queens and working at Prunelle one day when rabbit was being prepared," explained Michel. "The rabbit heads were about to be thrown away, and I wanted to take them home to eat along with the rabbit I'd shot that morning. I was planning a special dinner for Cynthia. [Michel and Cynthia had just been introduced on a skiing trip several weeks prior.] So I saved four of the heads."

Cynthia, then a young apprentice at New Jersey's Chez Catherine, was naturally curious about what French chef Michel would choose to cook for her. She was surprised when she lifted the lid on the pot and found five bunny heads—and one body—neatly packed for future culinary exploits.

"Whoa! There were those little heads, with teeth and no eyes," Cynthia recalled. "I told Michel he was lucky that I was wasn't raised like most American girls who would have been shocked at the mere thought—not to mention the sight—of bunny brains for dinner."

Cynthia grew up near Harrisburg, Pennsylvania, with a tradition of deer hunting and a family heritage of German butchers to fortify her against the sight of dismembered rabbits. She graduated from the Culinary Institute of America in 1983 and in addition to her work at Chez Catherine did a formal apprenticeship at Le Cirque in New York City. While at Le Cirque, Cynthia had the opportunity to work for the restaurant's famed chef Alain Sailiac and also well-known chefs Roger Verger and Paul Bocuse. Later Cynthia worked as acting chef at Lola's and then executive chef of Audrone's restaurant.

But the rabbit heads had made a lasting impression and a very positive one at that. Michel and Cynthia married and became partners in Restaurant du Village.

"I don't hunt," Cynthia said. "But I do walk with Michel. I enjoy the beauty, fragrance, and seasonality of the fall. I am more interested in the butchering aspect of game than Michel is. The entire seasonal process brings a kind of newness. I love re-creating fall in the kitchen with such ingredients as roasted chestnuts and bolete mushroom soup, boned quail filled with a meat stuffing and quince sauce, and red deer venison sautéed and flamed with London gin."

Oh, the sensibilities were definitely there, I thought. What a wild game meal they would cook!

When Chet telephoned to invite Ed and I to the game dinner, he tried to explain how Michel cooked mallards.

"Well, he puts the whole friggin' duck in a vat of fat," Chet said.

Only he didn't say "friggin'" and confirmed for me that his descriptive powers were definitely limited to his watercolor renditions. Not a foodie phrase or M. F. K. Fisher figure of food speech in Chet. He simply shouldn't be allowed to describe food. I assumed Chet was actually trying to say that Michel made a *confit de canard* out of the mallards. Of course, a confit is usually a perfect technique for the very fatty, domestic ducks or geese because the meat is cooked in its own fat. Fat is something domestic birds have a lot of, but wild birds are basically devoid of fat.

So now there was the bunny brain meal and a confit with ducks that didn't have fat. And then there was Michel's recipe for woodcock: Pluck the entire bird, including the head, then bend the head into the body so the beak skewers its waist. And bake. Well, it was something like that, I was hung up on visualizing the "skewering" and missed the cooking details. I also wondered, "Do you eat the brains and entrails?"

"Sometimes I make a paste from the entrails, but I try to think about who it is that is eating," explained Michel. "Some can't tolerate even the head and eyes of a fish being left on much less eating woodcock brain and entrails."

I wondered nervously how I would be evaluated on this scale of game-eating adventurousness.

The night of the Reneson game dinner arrived, a festive evening with a large guest list and best of all lots of game: venison, partridge, woodcock, quail, several species of ducks, goose, salmon, and trout. It had been a very good year. Michel and Cynthia arrived with no sign of a confit (she explained later to me that they add fat from domestic ducks to make a wild duck confit; a very tasty way to tenderize and preserve the sometimes tough wild ducks) and no sundry animal parts, just the duck breasts ready to grill. But the duck was accompanied by Michel's secret ingredient: a large jar filled with a bright red liquid with small floating balls in it. It look ominous; my mind was awhirl.

Michel sautéed the breasts quickly and began to make a sauce with the red stuff. Dare I ask?

"Cherries marinated in kirsch, for a long time," replied Michel.

Yes, he had definitely understood the temperament of this crowd. It was fabulous.

Black Duck with Sour Cherries in Kirsch Eau de Vie

(SERVES 4)

2 medium parsnips, peeled

2 medium carrots, peeled

2 medium turnips, peeled

2 black ducks, whole, plucked and cleaned

Salt

Freshly ground black pepper

1 tablespoon chopped fresh thyme leaves

2 garlic cloves, finely minced

1 cup sour cherries marinated for several months in Kirsch eau de vie (available in some gourmet shops or see recipe below), pitted and with juice

Vegetable oil

1 medium onion, peeled, quartered, and thickly sliced

1 cup reduced unsalted chicken broth

Preheat the oven to 400 degrees. Cut the parsnips, carrots, and turnips into a thick julienne about 1/4 inch square and 2 inches long. Rinse out the cavity of each duck with cold water and pat dry with paper towels. Season the ducks generously inside and out with salt and pepper. Rub about half of the thyme into the skin and place the remaining thyme along with the garlic into the cavity of the ducks. Add four or five cherries to the cavity.

Pour a small amount of oil into a heavy-bottomed ovenproof skillet and place over a medium-high heat. Brown the ducks in the oil, breast side down first, turning constantly until the ducks are entirely golden brown. Remove to a warm platter. Next lightly brown the parsnips, carrots, turnips, and onions in the same pan as the ducks, adding more oil if necessary. Place the ducks back in the pan atop the vegetables and put into the preheated oven for approximately 30 minutes. Check for doneness with an instant read thermometer. The internal temperature should be no more than 140 degrees.

Remove the ducks from the pan to a warm platter. Surround the ducks with the roasted vegetables. Pour 1/4 cup of the cherry juice into the skillet and place it over medium high heat. Scrape any brown bits with a wooden spoon to add flavor to the sauce. Tip the platter carefully, pouring any of the juices that have exuded from the duck into the pan. Now add the broth and reduce by half. Finally add the remaining cherries and simmer gently to warm the cherries.

Cut the ducks in half with poultry shears. Apportion one duck half per person surrounded by the roasted vegetables and with the cherry sauce served on the side.

This duck dish is particularly good accompanied by wild rice.

■ ■ ■

Sour Cherries in Kirsch Eau de Vie

Several pounds ripe sour cherries, stemmed
Kirsch eau de vie

Place the cherries in a large open-mouthed jar. Cover the cherries completely with Kirsch eau de vie. (This is a 90-proof unsweetened cherry brandy from the Alsace region of France.) Keep the cherries submerged in the brandy for several months, turning them occasionally to expose them evenly to the brandy.

The cherries and their juice may also be served in a small glass with a spoon after dinner.

Grouse with Sauerkraut

(SERVES 4)

Sauerkraut

2 packages fresh vacuum-packed
   sauerkraut (2 pounds each)

2 cups dry white wine

1 quart chicken stock

2 medium carrots, peeled and
   quartered lengthwise

1 large leek, dark greens removed,
   cut in half lengthwise

2 stalks celery, halved

12 juniper berries

3 bay leaves

8 peppercorns

Strain off all liquid brine from the sauerkraut and discard the brine. Rinse with cold water. Place in a large non-reactive bowl and cover with cold water. Soak 1/2 hour or longer. Drain the water, rinse, cover with more cold water, and soak for another 1/2 hour. Drain well.

Place the sauerkraut in a large Dutch oven and add all remaining ingredients. Place on the stove and bring to a boil and then reduce to a gentle simmer. Simmer covered 1 1/2–2 hours, stirring occasionally. (Be careful not to let the sauerkraut go dry or it will burn. If it starts to go dry, add water.) Remove from the heat and keep warm. You can make the sauerkraut 1 to 2 days in advance and keep it in the refrigerator, reheating when needed.

■ ■ ■

Grouse

4 dressed grouse (about 1 pound
   each)

Salt

Pepper

6 juniper berries, crushed

12 thin slices bacon

1 bunch fresh sage leaves

4 garlic cloves, smashed

3 cups of 1-inch chopped mire-
    poix vegetables (such as 2
    medium onions, 1 large carrot,
    and 2 stalks celery)

1 jigger gin
1 cup dry white wine
3 cups chicken stock

Rinse the grouse in cold running water and pat dry with paper towels. Check for and remove any visible shot pellets. Season the birds inside
and out with salt and pepper. Sprinkle the juniper inside the cavity of
each bird. Wrap each bird with 3 slices of bacon, being sure to cover the
breast area. Secure with wooden toothpicks. Place a few sage leaves and
1 clove of garlic in the cavity of each bird.

Preheat the oven to 450 degrees. Spray the bottom of a large roasting
pan with a nonstick spray. Spread the mirepoix vegetables evenly on
the bottom of the roasting pan. Place the birds breast up on top of the
vegetables, leaving space between each bird. Place the birds in the preheated oven and brown for 15 minutes. Reduce the heat to 375 degrees
and continue roasting for 15 minutes. Turn the birds over so that they
are resting on their breasts and finish roasting for 15 minutes.

Remove the pan from the oven. Gently lift the birds from the pan and
pour back any juices that may have collected in the cavities. Place the birds on
a platter and keep warm. Place the roasting pan on a burner and brown the
vegetables to make a pan sauce. Pour off any fat that may have collected in
the pan. Remove the pan from the heat and carefully add the gin to flambé,
return to the burner and tip pan to ignite if over an open flame or light with
a match. Douse the flame with the wine and add the stock. Bring to a boil.
Reduce until you have 1 cup of liquid, using a wooden spoon to loosen any
bits from the bottom. Strain the vegetables from the sauce and discard them.

Using a slotted spoon, place a generous portion of the sauerkraut in
the middle of each plate, to make a nest. Sit one bird in each nest. Spoon
some of the sauce over each bird, and serve the rest at the table.

*Accompany this meal with buttered steamed new potatoes, a loaf of crusty French
bread, and a bottle of dry Riesling wine from Alsace, France.*

Loup de Mer aux Morilles Sauce Pinot Noir

(SERVES 4)

Oil

1 pound sea bass trimmings (bones, skin, and belly flap with the exception of any red meat)

1 cup red table wine

2 shallots, thinly sliced

1 generous sprig thyme

1 quart unsalted chicken broth

2 tablespoons unsalted butter

8 ounces fresh morel mushrooms or 1 ounce dried morel mushrooms soaked in 1 cup warm water for 1/2 hour, halved

1 shallot, finely minced

Salt

Pepper

16 wild leeks (a.k.a. ramps) or 8 scallions

4 portions sea bass, cleaned of any dark meat (6 ounces each)

1 tablespoon canola oil or olive oil

Preheat the oven to 375 degrees. Lightly oil a roasting pan. Place the fish trimmings in the pan and bake in the preheated oven for 1/2 hour until golden brown.

In a non-reactive saucepan, place the red wine, the 2 thinly sliced shallots, and the thyme. Simmer approximately 15 minutes until the wine has reduced to a quarter of its original volume. Add the roasted fish trimmings and broth. Simmer until the volume is reduced by half. Strain the liquid into a smaller saucepot.

Melt 1/2 tablespoon of the butter in a small sauté pan. Add the mushrooms and gently sauté for about 5 minutes. Add the minced shallot and salt and pepper to taste and sauté for 2 to 3 minutes more. Remove from the heat and keep warm.

Trim roots off the leeks or scallions. Trim the greens so that the length of the greens is equal to that of the white portion of the leek. Melt 1/2 tablespoon of the butter in another small sauté pan. Sauté the leeks or scallions for about 5 minutes until tender. Season with salt and pepper to taste. Remove from the heat and keep warm.

Lightly salt and pepper the bass. Heat a heavy-bottomed, nonstick sauté pan on high heat. Add the oil and then carefully place the bass in the pan. Reduce the heat to medium-high heat and brown the bass on one side for 3 minutes. Turn the fish over gently and brown on other side for an additional 3 minutes.

While the fish is cooking, simmer the sauce until reduced by half. Whisk the remaining tablespoon butter and season with salt and pepper to taste.

Place one portion of the finished bass in the center of each plate. Divide the mushrooms and leeks evenly and place on each plate surrounding the bass. Spoon on the sauce to lightly cover the plate. Serve the remaining sauce on the side.

Josef Baron Kerckerinck zur Borg

Venison Purveyor and Owner, Lucky Star Ranch
Chaumont, New York

It was surprising to find Josef Baron Kerckerinck zur Borg aboard a scuba diving boat in the waters off Harbour Island, Bahamas. It's simply not where I'd expected to come across the titled German and founder of the first commercial deer farm in North America.

In the 1980s, "Jupp" (sounds like "yup") had come into the *Gray's Sporting Journal* periphery when he'd hired our magazine's art director, Larry Taylor, to design his book *Deer Farming in North America*, River Press (September, 1987). For a long time, Jupp was sort of fabled around *Gray's* as an exotically accented voice on the phone or as a dashing, confident aristocrat in a photo, touring his 4,500-acre Lucky Star estate in New York, a black Lab named Zulu riding atop the hood of the very cool, World War II–style Army jeep.

Now, in the Bahamas and in the flesh, Jupp was just one of several folks inelegantly dressed in fins, skins, and rubber hoses. Yes, a bit surprising. But at first take perhaps no more incongruent than featuring a baron in a cooking article. So how does a former German banker and advertising executive, the first purveyor of fresh venison to the restaurants of New York City, and a race car driver come to be part of a book about chefs? Well, the man can really cook.

Born in Germany during the rise of Nazism, Jupp grew up in the province of Westphalia, near Muenster, in a castle that had been the family home since 1466. He was his parents' sixth child, and at his birth Jupp's mother was awarded the Fuehrer's gold medal commending her on producing six Arian children. Incensed, she returned the medal saying she was "not a cow to be given premiums for her calves." She did not like the Nazis and her open hatred got her into trouble with the SS—and even stints in prison.

"She was a good cook but came home for meals at varying hours," Jupp recalled. "We had no modern conveniences—no central heating or hot water—to aid her in food preparation, so often she would leave half-prepared meals for me to complete. This is how I learned to cook."

Learning to hunt was a more formal process.

"I shot my first rabbit and pheasant at the age of twelve, my first roebuck at fourteen," Jupp said. "Although I had seen a deer earlier, I was too scared to pull the trigger and very happy no one was around to see it. In Europe, there are many rituals and rules to a hunt. We must age the animal we select to shoot, determine the age visually from body shape—the size of the pot belly and slope of the back—the antlers, and behavior. When a deer is taken, two boughs are broken from a tree. One is placed in the animal's mouth, representing its last meal, and the other is put on the hunter's hat, so the others will know his feat."

The formal shoot concludes with a bonfire and torch lighting by the members of the hunt and accompanied by a final blare of the hunter's horn to honor the slain animal. Jupp brought this *letzte bissen* and other European hunting traditions with him when he immigrated to the United States in 1978.

When the eldest Kerckerinck brother sold the family estate, Jupp, as manager of the property, needed a new job. Jupp was uninterested in returning to either of his previous banking or advertising careers and decided—given the expensive real estate prices in Germany—to create his own domain in the United States. He first purchased a 1,500-acre parcel near Chaumont in the Thousand Island region of New York and launched Lucky Star Ranch as a venison farm, raising fallow deer for New York City restaurants.

New York chefs are notoriously attached to their purveyors and it was difficult initially to convert them from New Zealand–raised venison to the New York state deer. But Jupp knew marketing and had a flair for the theatrical. Dressed elegantly in black-tie, he drove to Manhattan with a fresh deer carcass in the back of his Chevy Blazer and began knocking on the kitchen doors of the best restaurants, offering to provide the chefs with their choice of venison cuts instantly.

Jupp founded the North American Deer Farming Association whose members today include more than 4,000 deer farms in the United States and Canada. And he added land to his Lucky Star Ranch. But his growth also brought meat processing problems and heavy restrictions from the USDA on exactly what he could sell. Six years ago, Jupp decided to stop venison farming.

"A lot of people asked to hunt here," Jupp said. "And I said to myself, why not? It should be a good business. And as it turned out, it is."

In 1999, Lucky Star Ranch became a premier hunting and fishing preserve. Of course, Lucky Star offers excellent deer hunting. Five species—European fallow deer, red stag, sika deer, North American whitetail, and elk-size Pere David deer (native to China)—are available to hunt in a fenced 1,400-acre area. Additionally, there is a 1,500-acre enclosure just for whitetails and a 1,600-acre tract that's part of the property but unfenced and posted for free-roaming whitetails.

And now because of Jupp's extensive habitat management, guided hunts for wild turkey and waterfowl on the ranch's one hundred-acre lake—where, too, there is fishing for bass, northern pike, and panfish—are also available. But to augment the European flavor of the experience, Jupp offers classic driven pheasant hunts where dogs and beaters flush birds toward shotgunners posted in stands. Rough, or "walk-up," hunts are also offered, but the driven pheasant hunt is Jupp's specialty. He starts the shoot with three quick blasts on a brass horn and a plunge into the brush with Zulu, several other dogs, and the beaters.

Jupp seems to be able to do it all. He's guide, host, beater, dog handler, wildlife manager, and farmer—and last but certainly never in this cookbook least, game chef. Certainly such emphasis on the gastronomic, the elegance of place and particularly the dining room, and the attention paid to proper game presentation and preparation indicates a true connoisseur of the sporting life.

Sliced Duck Breast in Cumberland Sauce

(SERVES 4)

2 cups currant jelly

2 tablespoons Worcestershire sauce

1/4 cup red vinegar

2 tablespoons Dijon mustard

1 teaspoon ground cumin

1/2 cup port wine

1 tablespoon orange zest

1 tablespoon lemon zest

1/4 cup fresh orange juice

1/4 cup fresh lemon juice

1/2 cup finely chopped shallots

1 tablespoon dry mustard

2 teaspoons ground ginger

2 teaspoons ground black pepper

1/2 teaspoon salt

4 duck breasts

Oil or butter

Mix all ingredients except the duck and oil or butter together in a saucepan and heat on medium heat until the jelly has melted. Let stand for at least 30 minutes.

In a large skillet, sauté the duck for 2 to 3 minutes on each side in oil or butter. Slice into 1/4-inch thick slices on the diagonal.

(You can prepare the sauce and duck in advance. Place the cooked duck in aluminum foil to keep hot. Shortly before serving, put them back into the pan for about 1 minute, turning them immediately once they are in the pan. Take out and serve with reheated sauce.)

This recipe goes well with rice or potatoes and vegetables.

Tenderloin, Watercress, Fennel, and Orange Salad

(SERVES 4)

1 tablespoon fresh ginger
1/4 cup orange juice
1 teaspoon fresh orange zest
2 tablespoons olive oil
Black pepper
8–10 ounces venison tenderloin
1 handful watercress
1/2 head red leaf lettuce
1 bulb fennel, sliced
2 oranges, peeled and thinly sliced
1 avocado, sliced
1 tablespoon lemon juice
Dressing (see recipe below)

In a large bowl, combine the ginger, orange juice, orange zest, oil, and pepper. Wrap the venison in aluminum foil with the marinade and seal tightly. Marinate the tenderloin for 1 hour.

Preheat the oven to 325 degrees. Place the venison in the preheated oven and bake 10 minutes. (The meat should be pink inside.)

Slice the venison into thin slices. Place the watercress, lettuce, and fennel on plates. Arrange the orange slices in a circle with the tenderloin slices on top. Place the avocado slices on either side and sprinkle with lemon juice. Drizzle dressing (see recipe below) over it and serve.

Dressing

4 tablespoons olive oil
1/4 cup orange juice
1/2 tablespoons balsamic vinegar
1 teaspoon fresh ginger

In a bowl, combine the oil, orange juice, vinegar, and ginger.

This delicious recipe was given to the Lucky Star Ranch by the honorable Leora Hamilton, who is a great friend and a great cook!

Stock Reduction with Juniper Essence

(MAKES 3 CUPS)

Bones and trimmings
Olive oil
1 medium leek, chopped
1 stalk celery, chopped
3 medium onions, chopped
2 cups mushrooms (shiitake, oyster, or portobello)
1 medium parsnip, chopped
1 cup red wine
4 garlic cloves
Bouquet Garni (see recipe below)
2 tablespoons tomato paste
1/4 cup juniper berries
3/4 cup gin

Preheat the oven to 450 degrees. Oil the bones and trimmings and put them in a roasting pan. Bake the bones and trimmings in the preheated oven until brown. Then add the leek, celery, onions, mushrooms, and parsnips and cook until well browned.

Transfer the bones and vegetables to a large stock pot. Deglaze the roasting pan with the wine and add the mixture to the pot. Cover the bones and vegetables with water, add the garlic, and simmer for several hours until the liquid is reduced to about 20 percent.

Now add the Bouquet Garni (see recipe below) and the tomato paste. Let simmer for another 1/2 hour, or until the stock is reduced to approximately 3 cups.

Place the juniper berries and the gin into a small saucepan and simmer until the alcohol is burned off. Combine the juniper berry essence with the stock and simmer until reduced to 2 cups. Strain it several times through a cheesecloth until clear. You can then place the stock into ice cube trays, let it cool off, and freeze it. Use the cubes as needed.

. . .

Bouquet Garni

1 tablespoon fresh thyme
12 parsley stems
1 tablespoon black peppercorns
4 bay leaves
1 tablespoon fresh oregano
4 garlic cloves, minced

In a bowl, combine all ingredients. Place in a sachet bag or cheesecloth or just add to the stock loose.

Smoked Salmon on Potato Pancakes with Horseradish Whipping Cream

(MAKES ABOUT 8 PIECES)

1/2 cup heavy cream
Horseradish sauce
4 potatoes
1 egg
Olive oil
8 slices smoked salmon
Lemon wedges

In a bowl, whip the cream until firm. Add the horseradish sauce to taste.

In another bowl, grate the potatoes coarsely. Mix the egg well into the potatoes and let stand for 10 minutes.

Heat a sauté pan with oil. Using a teaspoon, shape the potato mixture into small pancakes of 2 inches in diameter. Fry one side of the pancakes in oil until the edges brown and then turn to fry the other side. Put the pancakes on paper towels to drip off the excess oil and keep them warm.

Arrange the pancakes on a platter or plate and place slices of smoked salmon on top.

Add some horseradish whipping cream sauce and serve with wedges of lemon.

Variation: You can also mix some lingonberries into the horseradish whipping cream sauce.

Hungarian-Style Stuffed Onions

(SERVES 4)

4 yellow onions (each about the same size), peeled

2 tablespoons olive oil

1 teaspoon minced garlic

1 tablespoon paprika

Pinch cumin

1/2 pound venison, ground or finely chopped

1 tablespoon salt

1 green bell pepper, sliced and finely chopped

1 tomato, sliced

1 cup water

Salt

Sour cream

Cut a thin slice off the bottom and 1-inch slice off the top of each onion. Scoop out the inside of each onion to make room for the stuffing. Finely chop the insides and reserve for the stuffing.

In a sauté pan, sauté the chopped onions in the oil until golden. Season with the garlic, paprika, and cumin to taste. Add the venison and salt and then cover and braise. (Brown in fat over high heat then cover tightly and cook slowly, adding 1/4 cup of water to get more juice.) Strain the venison when tender and remove from the pan. Add the bell pepper and tomato to the roasting juices and simmer gently at moderate heat for a few more minutes.

Place the onion shells in a single layer in a large pot with about 3/4 cups salted water. Cover the pot and cook the onions for about 30 minutes, until soft. Stuff the onion shells with the mixture of meat, pepper, and tomato and cook them for another 2 or 3 minutes.

Serve with a dollop of sour cream on top of each onion.

Pheasant Breast with Cinnamon and Orange Marmalade

(SERVES 8)

8 boneless pheasant breasts
4 tablespoons butter
9 tablespoons flour
1/2 tablespoon cinnamon
1 cup orange juice
4 tablespoons orange marmalade

1 1/2 tablespoons instant chicken broth
2 tablespoons orange liqueur
1 cup green seedless grapes
2 oranges, peeled and sectioned
1/2 cup toasted almonds

Preheat the oven to 325 degrees. Line an 8- by 8-inch baking pan (1/2 inch high) with aluminum foil, allowing the ends to be long enough so you can fold the foil over the top to seal it tightly. Wash the pheasant, pat dry with paper towels, and arrange in the baking pan.

In a saucepan, melt the butter over medium heat. Stir in the flour and cinnamon and cook until smooth. Stir in the orange juice, marmalade, and broth. Cook until thick, stirring constantly. Add the liqueur, stirring carefully. Spoon the mixture over the pheasant.

Seal the foil tightly and bake in the preheated oven for 15 minutes, or until the pheasant is tender. Remove the pheasant from the oven, place the grapes and orange sections on top of the pheasant, and bake uncovered for 5 more minutes. Sprinkle with the almonds.

This delicious recipe came to the Lucky Star Ranch courtesy of Lorie Hall.

Venison Loin with Green Peppercorns

(SERVES 4)

1 loin venison

2 tablespoons green peppercorns

2 tablespoons minced garlic

1/2 bottle of red wine (about 2 cups)

4 ounces mushrooms

Olive oil

2 tablespoons brandy

1/2 cup heavy cream

Salt

Pepper

Trim any fat off the venison and cut it into 1-inch-thick medallions. Place the venison in a baking dish. Add the peppercorns and garlic and cover with the wine. Let stand for at least 1 hour. (You can do this the day before.)

Drain the marinade, reserving the peppercorns and garlic. In a skillet, sauté the peppercorns and garlic for 1 minute and add the mushrooms. Remove and hold. Add the oil to the skillet. Sauté the venison, searing it on both sides (2 1/2 minutes for rare, 3 1/2 minutes for medium). Remove the venison from the skillet and keep it warm in aluminum foil.

Heat the brandy in the skillet, allowing it to boil for a minute. Add the cream and reduce until slightly thickened. Add the peppercorns, garlic, and mushrooms and season to taste with salt and pepper. Add the venison and juices to the sauce. Serve immediately.

This delicious recipe came to the Lucky Star Ranch courtesy of the honorable Leora Hamilton.

Saddle of Venison

(SERVES 6 TO 8)

1 saddle venison*
Salt
Pepper
2 onions, quartered
1/2 pound carrots
2 tomatoes, chopped
12 juniper berries, crushed

2 bay leaves
8 tablespoons butter
2 cups red wine
Heavy cream
Cranberry jelly
Sour cream

Preheat the oven to 375 degrees. Clean the venison from any silver skin on the loins to expose the red meat. Place the venison in a roasting pan and sprinkle with salt and pepper. Put the onions, carrots, tomatoes, juniper berries, and bay leaves around the venison.

In a skillet, melt the butter. Pour the butter over the venison. Pour 1 cup of the wine over the venison.

Bake the venison in the preheated oven, basting every 10 minutes with the juices from the roasting pan. After about 30 minutes (depending on how you like the meat; venison should not be well done but rather pink), take the venison out of the roasting pan and wrap it in aluminum foil. Let it rest for 10 to 15 minutes.

Meanwhile deglaze the roasting pan, keeping all the vegetables in it, with the remaining 1 cup of wine and bring to a boil. Scrape carefully along the bottom of pan, strain into smaller pot, and let it boil for a few minutes more. Then add some cream, cranberry jelly, and sour cream. (Don't let the mixture boil anymore after you've added the sour cream and heavy cream.)

Carefully carve the two loins off the bone in one piece each. Take the loins and cut them into 1-inch-thick slices and place them back on the bone. (This makes a very interesting and unusual presentation.)

Add the juices that drained from the venison while carving into the sauce in the roasting pan to add flavor to the sauce.

Serve the saddle on the bone with the sauce on the side.

This dish tastes great with red cabbage and potatoes or pasta like spaetzle.

* Note: A saddle is the back of the deer, both loins on the bone and the ribs cut off with a bone saw, directly underneath the loins. The old wisdom is that the meat next to the bone tastes the best, and therefore we like to cook it with the bones.

Doug Mack and Linda Harmon

Chef and Co-owners,
The Inn at Baldwin Creek and Mary's Restaurant
Bristol, Vermont

Most of the chefs in this book came to game cooking because they were either hunters or heavily schooled in the traditionally game-inclusive cuisines of Europe—or both. But Doug Mack's route to game cookery was different.

"I see food as a venue for change and feel it is important to connect Vermont's small farms to restaurants," Doug said. He talks the Alice Waters' talk—an environmentally conscious chef who buys both seasonally and regionally—and walks that walk as well. Doug is a founding member of The Vermont Fresh Network—a statewide organization dedicated to promoting small Vermont farmers by making that connection to restaurants. And he's spent twenty years now creating partnerships with local producers, family farmers, and foragers, partnerships that include every product from Vermont Butter & Cheese goat cheese, lamb from Old Chatham Sheepherding Company, Phil Brown's Cavendish Game Birds, and Joe Messina's (see page 132) Adventure in Food boar and buffalo. What makes Doug exceptional in the artisanal, fresh food movement is that he sees farm-raised game as a critical piece in the spectrum of buying from local farmers and maintaining the food sensibilities of the region.

I had heard first about Doug and his wife, Linda Harmon, in the context of their seasonal events. As co-owners of The Inn at Baldwin Creek and Mary's

Restaurant in Bristol, Vermont, the couple has been very creative in involving their customers not just in dinners but in full culinary experiences.

"Nowadays people want to know more about where their food comes from and be adventuresome in their eating," said Doug.

So every Wednesday night in the spring and summer, Mary's Restaurant offers Farmhouse Dinners where locally raised products, along with the corresponding farmers, are showcased. Guests have an opportunity to meet, mingle, and listen to the farmers who grow these wonderful products. Linda and Doug also offer a Vermont Fresh Farm Package: a stay at the Inn with days spent visiting Vermont farms and nights spent dining on what you've seen growing. The package can include cooking classes as well.

But of course what intrigued me was the fall event at Mary's—a series of three wine and game dinners in November. Ed and I were invited to spend the night at the Inn and attend the third and final dinner for the year.

"A little out of the way . . . a lot out of the ordinary." That's the descriptor on the printed and Web site material for the Inn at Baldwin Creek. Certainly the former was immediately apparent and somewhat of an understatement. The old New England mill, turned home and dairy farm, turned inn, was still settled on 25 acres—with a driveway that once had been the main road to Burlington—and *was* out of the way. But any inconvenience was justifiable—we thought necessary and well worth it—for to preserve the beauty and serenity of what once was, nowadays it better be a bit hard to get there.

The cold fall evening was heavy and dark, and dried remnants of the bountiful herb and perennial flower gardens recalled summer's lusciousness at the Inn at Baldwin Creek. Yet the mellow warmth of indoors and the smell of wood smoke invited us inside, and we were happy to not only be dining on game but spending more than mealtime at the Inn.

Like many vintage 1797 farmhouses, the downstairs rooms rambled horizontally, like telescoping boxes, and our culinary experience would drift from the large central room with the bar, through one dining room, and then to the very back where six or seven tables were intimately arranged near a fireplace. We sampled boar and buffalo sausage with cranberry ketchup and horseradish mustard while sipping a Fontella Chianti '01, and then we were shown to our table, next to the fireplace. Our appetizer was a venison pâté with a maple mustard and pickled onions, followed by mixed greens with a cave-ripened Colby cheese and grilled quail tossed in a lime vinaigrette. Then came the main courses: first herb and pepper encrusted sautéed antelope medallions and then grilled kangaroo steak with a roasted garlic and thyme sauce. And in case we thought we were done with heavenly foods, then arrived the dessert of pear and dried cherry tartlet topped with hazelnut whipped cream! Between each course, the wine host—Joerg Klauck—and Joe Messina—the game host—spoke about the different game dishes and pairing with the various wines.

Interestingly, our real host—Chef Doug Mack—never made an appearance and never announced the dishes. It was almost like he preferred to keep the ingredients—rather than his recipes and cooking techniques—center stage for the evening. Of course this exceptional meal for 50 people kept Doug quite exceptionally busy in the kitchen, too. And would there be time and opportunity after dinner at the bar, with Cognac in hand, to talk about his art? Probably not, and after a meal like that how could I possibly keep my mind on clear and impartial journalism? I had been to culinary heaven and wasn't ready to come back to earth.

In the morning we breakfasted with Joe Messina and then over a second cup of coffee talked with Doug and Linda.

"I think it was in the stars that I'd become a chef," Doug said as he recalled his first job in a restaurant. "I was a dishwasher in high school. The cook quit one day unexpectedly and I was offered the job. Often you move up the ladder in kitchens when someone—the cook—just doesn't show one day."

Doug went to Ohio University and studied photography, worked in a pizzeria, and spent his time in a cycle of studying, cooking, and shooting photos. He graduated in 1977 and then returned to his hometown in Basking Ridge, New Jersey. He continued to photograph and cook. His days were spent photographing—evenings he worked at a family-style restaurant named The Store as a line-cook, eventually advancing to their head chef position. And he dreamed not only of producing picture books but making creative, interesting food. After a year it was the cooking that more and more filled and fulfilled Doug's time. He met Linda, who was general manager at another restaurant, and their partnership seemed a natural on many levels.

In 1980, Doug and Linda began looking for a business they could do on their own. They wanted a life style change, too, and when a young and close friend died of cancer, they felt a new sense of urgency to reach goals and realize dreams. Do it now, not later. In 1982, they moved to Charlotte, Vermont, not far from Burlington, and took jobs at the Sirloin Saloon in "front of the house" positions—Doug was the bar manager—while they looked for a business to buy. When tending bar one evening, Doug heard there was a storefront restaurant for sale in Bristol, and in 1983 they bought Mary's. A 50-seat vegetarian restaurant, Doug and Linda would alter "little" Mary's—as they call it to differentiate it from its successor—making it neighborhood-bar-friendly and changing the menu to encompass all cuisines, and they included fish and game.

"A Vermont venue should serve game," Doug explained. "The state combines a rural population that is used to eating game with people who are well traveled and interested in experimenting with regional foods."

Doug spent the next ten years building his relationships with the local farmers, foragers, and purveyors.

"We worked like crazy," he said. And in 1993, their success enabled them to expand, buying the Inn at Baldwin Creek, moving Mary's restaurant, and offering lodging, dining, catered events, and weddings. During the 1990s, Doug and Linda rounded out their offerings at the Inn with cooking classes, theme meals like Flyfishing Father's Day Brunch, and the coupling of farm tours with dining. In 1998, they held their first game dinner series. Wine and game connoisseurs were asked to speak and mingle with guests during the evening, providing not just information about the various dishes but giving the event personality.

"We had always served game at Mary's," Doug said. "Of course, we were sensitive to the obvious no-no's—like don't serve rabbit for an Easter dinner—but now we wanted a seasonal event that centered on game and would introduce a sophisticated, adventuresome audience to new, out-of-the-ordinary foods. We wanted to reach beyond our usual venison burger, give the guests the opportunity to try something they wouldn't usually eat."

"Ah," I said, "thus your reasoning for serving kangaroo last night."

Doug shifted uneasily in his chair and said: "Well, unfortunately the feedback on the kangaroo was that it made diners uncomfortable, something about the image of eating a cute kangaroo. It's the same problem people have with trying bear."

I guess Bambi is one thing to a Vermonter, but the Pooh and Roo connection is another. Or it just may be that "a lot out of the ordinary" is fine, just don't go to Australia to find it. The extraordinary is best found right at home.

Venison Pâté

2 1/4 pounds ground venison
1/4 pounds ground pork
1 cup bread crumbs
3 cups milk
3 eggs
3 tablespoons chopped parsley

1 teaspoon thyme
1 ounce brandy
1 teaspoon chopped parsley
12 slices bacon
Maple Mustard Sauce (see recipe below)

In a medium bowl, mix all ingredients together except for the bacon and Maple Mustard Sauce. Line a loaf pan with the bacon, fill with the meat mixture. Cover the bread pan with foil and place in a roasting pan. Fill the roasting pan halfway up with water. Bake for 1 1/2 hours, or until an instant-read thermometer 145 degrees. Take the pâté out of the water bath and chill at least 5 hours before serving. Serve with Maple Mustard Sauce (see recipe below).

. . .

Maple Mustard Sauce

3/4 cup Dijon mustard or whole grain mustard
1/2 cup maple syrup

In a medium bowl, combine the mustard and maple syrup and mix until smooth.

Antelope and Eggplant Curry

(SERVES 4)

2 tablespoons oil
1/2 cup red onion, finely chopped
20 ounces antelope leg meat, cubed
2 cups of peeled, diced eggplant
Sauce (see recipe below)
Rice, cooked

In a medium saucepan, heat the oil. Add the onion and antelope and sauté until the meat is browned and the onion is clear, about 5 minutes. Add the eggplant and then the Sauce (see recipe below). Simmer over low heat for another 15 minutes. Serve over rice.

■ ■ ■

Sauce

4 ounces butter
2 tablespoons flour
1/4 cup soy sauce
1/4 cup maple syrup
1 cup ketchup

1 cup red wine
1/4 cup brandy
1 teaspoon Dijon mustard
1 tablespoon curry powder

In a medium saucepan, melt the butter. When melted, add the flour, stirring constantly for 3 to 4 minutes. Then add the remaining ingredients. Simmer for 15 minutes, transfer to a blender, and puree until smooth.

Vermont Rabbit Cooked in Hard Cider with Apples

(SERVES 4)

1 cup flour

1 teaspoon salt

1 teaspoon pepper

1 teaspoon paprika

1 rabbit (3 pounds), cut into sections and the carcass reserved for the stock

3 tablespoons olive oil

2 Granny Smith apples, cut into wedges

Stock (see recipe below)

2 cups hard cider

1/2 cup heavy cream or crème fraîche

1 tablespoon tomato paste

In a shallow bowl, combine the flour, salt, pepper, and paprika. Coat the rabbit pieces in the flour mixture, shaking off any extra. Set aside.

In a large frying pan, heat the oil over medium heat until hot, but not smoking. Add the rabbit pieces and cook 3 minutes. Turn and cook until browned, 3 minutes more. Add the apples and sauté briefly. Add the Stock (see recipe below) and hard cider. Simmer for 30 minutes.

Add the cream and tomato paste, simmer 15 minutes being careful not to bring the mixture to a boil. Place the rabbit on a platter and spoon the sauce over it.

• • •

Stock

4 quarts water
1 celery stick, coarsely chopped
1 carrot, coarsely chopped
1 medium onion, cut into quarters
Trimmed rabbit bones (reserved from above)

In a medium stockpot simmer the water, celery, carrot, onion, and the rabbit bones. Bring to a boil and allow to simmer until the mixture has reduced to a quart, about 1 1/2 hours. Strain the stock and reserve. (This can be made ahead of time.)

Vermont Pheasant Cooked with Sundried Bing Cherry and Applejack Brandy Sauce

(SERVES 2)

1 cup white wine
1/2 cup oil
1 teaspoon tarragon
1 teaspoon chopped garlic
1 teaspoon chopped parsley
1 pheasant, plucked, cleaned, legs and breasts removed
White wine
Sundried Bing Cherry and Applejack Brandy Sauce (see recipe below)
Oil

In a large bowl, combine the wine, 1/2 cup oil, tarragon, garlic, and parsley. Marinate the pheasant breasts and legs for 1 hour before cooking.

Preheat the oven to 350 degrees. Roast the marinated breasts and legs in a little wine for about 15 minutes in the preheated oven. Remove the breasts; roast the legs for another 15 minutes. Keep the breasts and legs in a warm place while making the Sundried Bing Cherry and Applejack Brandy Sauce (see recipe below).

In a pan, sauté the breasts in a small amount of oil, heating the oil until hot before adding the breasts to avoid sticking to the bottom of the pan. Cook the breasts 3 minutes per side.

Slice the breasts in thin strips cut on the bias, place in a small pool of sauce and fan out. Prior to serving, reheat the legs in the oven for 10 minutes. Serve the leg alongside the sliced breasts.

• • •

Sundried Bing Cherry and Applejack Brandy Sauce

1/2 cup sundried cherries (soaked for 4 hours in warm water) or fresh
   cherries
1 cup mushrooms
1 ounce oil or butter
1/2 cup applejack brandy
1 teaspoon flour
1 1/2 cups chicken stock
1 tablespoon chopped parsley

Sauté the cherries and the mushrooms in the oil. When the mushrooms are soft, add the brandy. After 1 minute, add the flour and simmer for 2 minutes, then add the stock and parsley and simmer for 15 minutes.

Bacon-Wrapped Venison Tenderloin with Red Wine Gorgonzola Sauce

(SERVES 4)

Venison has very little fat, so wrapping the fillet with bacon keeps the meat juicy and imparts a nice smoky taste to the meat.

4 venison tenderloin steaks (6 ounces each)
4 strips bacon
Red Wine Gorgonzola Sauce (see recipe below)

Wrap each steak with a strip of bacon. Secure the bacon slices with toothpicks. Grill or sauté the steaks much the same way you would cook a beef steak. Serve in a pool of Gorgonzola Sauce (see recipe below).

■ ■ ■

Gorgonzola Sauce

1/2 cup mushrooms
1 tablespoon oil
1 teaspoon flour
1 cup beef or venison stock

1/4 pound Gorgonzola cheese
1 cup red wine
1 teaspoon basil

In a saucepan, simmer the mushrooms in the oil. Add the flour and then the remaining ingredients. Simmer until smooth and thick.

John Manikowski

Restaurateur, Chef, Cookbook Author, and Artist
Mill River, Massachusetts

"No chef can live in a void" is John Manikowski's mantra, although the product of his devotion—wild game cookery—hardly needs the emphasis of a chant. John has beautifully blended his abilities as fine artist and culinary wizard with his hunting and fishing, successfully confirming not only that he lives in no void but that his cuisine has a spirit.

Born in Minnesota, 250 miles from Minneapolis and just down the road from Fargo, North Dakota, in what he describes as "truly the land of 10,000 lakes," John fished for rock bass, perch, and anything else that lived in the border rivers of the Bois de Sioux and Red River of the North. As a twelve-year-old, John first learned upland shooting from his brother-in-law. And perhaps in classic kid-memory hyperbole, John recalls taking home "truckloads" of pheasants—assuredly there were higher limits then.

After finishing college, John took advantage of the free-travel perk from his railroad engineer father, flipped a coin east or west, and in 1965 headed to the Northeast. He attended graduate school at Rhode Island School of Design and taught in and around the Boston area until a grant from the National Endowment for the Arts allowed him to move to the Berkshires in western Massachusetts. Continuing to paint and teach, John purchased an old, run-down, 32-room hotel in Mill River not far from the resort area of Great Barrington.

At first, John ran just a small catering business out of the building, where he also lived. The business eventually evolved into a storefront deli and take-out. Then a couple tables and chairs were added. By 1982, it had developed into a full-fledged restaurant with low lighting and seating for 40 to 50 diners. It was called Konkapot after the Indian chief and his namesake Konkapot River, which flowed in front of the restaurant.

Over time, the Konkapot fare came to include prix fixe game dinners—a different menu for each month in the fall, with the venison, quail, and pheasant procured from specialty meat purveyors. The menus always reflected John's experience with wild ingredients and nature. In time, Native American foods and techniques were even incorporated—roasted buffalo steak or planked salmon and various smoked meats.

Konkapot grew and flourished until the bridge crossing the river was condemned, cutting off ready access to the restaurant for nearly four years while the state re-built the bridge. But with the bad came some good. At about the same time Konkapot's business began to decline, a woman from Manhattan named Carol Clark approached John about opening another restaurant. She'd done catering in New York but wanted to move out of the city to her country home and needed a partner. Carol and John opened Charleston in Hudson, New York. In 1987, John was running two restaurants—and going "crazy." He closed Konkapot and focused his attentions on Charleston.

Although during those years, John rarely wrote a recipe down, he described the process for developing the meals at his two restaurants:

"Always keep an open mind—I'd take cooking advice from the sixteen-year-old dishwasher if it was good—change the menu weekly, and regularly take field trips to other restaurants for ideas and inspiration."

Not living in a void as a cook produced some very sophisticated food combinations for John, especially with game, first for the restaurants and then finally relenting to write them down for his cookbook *Wild Fish & Game Cookbook*, Artisan (October, 1997) including Sautéed Caribou with Puffballs and Pears, Grilled Wild Boar Chops with Coconut-Lime Sauce, Grilled Quail with Mango and Peach Salsa, and my personal favorite, Basque-Style Pheasant with Olives.

"I like hunting, cooking, and eating poultry," John said. "Having grown up in a family that hunted and cooked ducks and pheasant all the time, it's just plain easy for me."

But too much of the unusual and unfamiliar can trigger culinary failure, John readily admits.

"The beavertail I grilled, sliced thin, and garnished the hell out of, tasted like. . ."

Well, you don't need much of an imagination to fill in the blank.

Several years ago, John decided to retire from the restaurant business—just filling in for Carol when he was needed—to focus exclusively on his writing and painting and, of course, on hunting and fishing, too. In April, 2004, his second cookbook was published. Entitled *Fish: Grilled & Smoked* (Storey Publishing), it contains not only fantastic recipes but is illustrated with around 30 of John's drawings. He has worked on publishing a murder mystery he wrote about a group of hunters who one by one get killed off by, what else, the food. He has taken up mushroom foraging and talks about spending the winter months in Mexico, painting and writing.

No longer spending hours early and late in the kitchen, John enjoys at least the dawn and dusk hours of duck season on the two ponds near his home.

"It's easy hunting," he said.

John takes his Walkman, a little Chopin on the tape, and a good library book and sits in the blind, waiting for the ducks.

Smoked Puffballs

puffball mushrooms, sliced into 1/2-inch by 2- to 3-inch pieces

Heat a smoker for 5 to 10 minutes or until the wood chips are smoking. Lay the mushrooms on the cool side of the smoker. Smoke at 250 degrees for about 1 hour, turning once.

Use these delicious mushrooms in tomato pasta sauce or as a flavoring in soup. Smoked/dried mushrooms will keep in a covered container indefinitely. You can reconstitute the mushrooms by soaking them in water, sherry, or Madeira for about 20 minutes.

Grilled Wood Duck with Dried Cherry Sauce

(SERVES 4)

1/4 cup olive oil
2 tablespoons lemon juice
1/4 cup fresh thyme, stemmed, or 2 teaspoons dried
1 teaspoon freshly ground black pepper
4 wood ducks or other wild ducks
1 1/4 cups dried cherries
2 tablespoons Triple Sec or brandy
1/2 cup orange juice
1 1/2 cups dry red wine
1/3 cup balsamic vinegar
1 1/2 cup unsalted veal or chicken stock
Zest of 1 orange

In a small bowl, combine the oil, lemon juice, thyme, and pepper and whisk together. Set aside.

Wash the ducks and pat dry them dry with paper towels. Split them up the back and lay them flat. Place the ducks in a non-reactive container large enough to just accommodate them and pour the marinade over. Cover and refrigerate for about 1 1/2 hours.

In a small bowl, soak the cherries in the Triple Sec or brandy and orange juice for about 25 minutes. Meanwhile, start a fire in a charcoal grill. In a medium saucepan over medium-high heat, combine the cherries and their juices with the wine. Bring to a boil, lower the heat, and simmer for 3 to 4 minutes, uncovered, until the cherries are soft. Add the vinegar and simmer for 2–3 minutes more. Add the stock and reduce by about half, cooking for 8 to 10 minutes. Remove from the heat and keep warm.

When the charcoal is gray and hot, remove the ducks from the marinade, shake off most of the excess, and place them on the grate. Grill for 4 to 5 minutes, turn and grill another 3 to 4 minutes for medium-rare to medium. (Add about 2 minutes on each side if you prefer your meat cooked more.) Remove the ducks from the grill, cut each duck up the breast bone, separating them in half, and lay a half on each of 4 warmed plates, breast up. Ladle cherry sauce over each, sprinkle orange zest over all, and serve immediately.

Serve with celeriac-laced mashed potatoes and sugar snap peas sautéed in butter with fresh thyme.

Fish, Corn, and Apple Chowder

(SERVES 4 TO 6)

8 ounces salt pork, skin removed

1 tablespoon canola oil or corn oil

1 medium sweet white onion, finely chopped (about 1 cup)

2 stalks celery, finely chopped (about 3/4 cup)

2 apples, peeled, cored, and chopped (about 1 cup)

2 medium potatoes, chopped

2 cups fish stock

2 cups milk

1 cup heavy cream

2 1/2 cups fresh corn kernels

1 pound firm whitefish fillets (such as bass, pike, or striped bass), cut into 1-inch cubes

3 tablespoons Old Bay Seasoning or paprika

1/2 teaspoon salt

1 teaspoon freshly ground pepper

1 tablespoon chives or scallions, finely chopped

1 red bell pepper, finely chopped

Bring 2 quarts water to a boil in a small saucepan and add the salt pork. Blanch over medium heat for 6 to 8 minutes to remove the excess salt and nitrates. Drain, cool, and chop the salt pork into 1/2-inch cubes.

In a large saucepan or stockpot, heat the oil over medium-high heat. Add the salt pork and fry for 10 to 12 minutes or until browned and crispy. Drain, reserving fat. Return 2 tablespoons of the fat to the pot and set the salt pork aside. Discard the excess fat. Add the onion, celery, and apples and sauté for 10 to 12 minutes. Add the potatoes and stock and simmer over medium heat for about 15 minutes.

In a small saucepan over medium heat, bring the milk and cream nearly to the boil but remove from heat before it begins boiling. Add to the large saucepan with the vegetables and stock. Add the corn, fish, browned salt pork, Old Bay Seasoning or paprika, salt, and pepper. Stir and simmer over low heat, never boiling, for about 15 minutes, covered. Add the chives or scallions. Remove from the heat and ladle into soup bowls. (Strain and remove the salt pork pieces if desired.) Serve immediately, garnished with the red pepper.

Wine Recommendation:

Vidgnier, a wine made from a unique grape of the same name, is affordable. It is made by Georges Duboeuf. This wine from the south of France is floral and aromatic enough to balance the fish and spices of this chowder.

Or try Conundrum, a special wine made to match with seafood by red wine producer Caymus Vineyards from California. The white wine is a blend of four or five different white grape varieties that is exceptionally floral, complex, and has a pleasant lingering finish.

Red and Blue Grilled and Smoked Arctic Char with Blueberry Balsamic Sauce

(SERVES 4)

Hardwood chips such as apple, cherry, or grapevines
1/2 stalk fresh fennel
2 pounds boneless arctic char (about 2 fillets)
2 cups fresh blueberries
1 cup low-sodium chicken stock
1/4 cup orange flavored liqueur such as Triple Sec or orange curaçao
1 tablespoon freshly squeezed lemon juice
1/4 cup fresh thyme, stemmed
2 tablespoons maple syrup
1 1/2 teaspoon balsamic vinegar

Preheat a wood fire or charcoal or gas grill. Lay out an 18-inch square of heavy-duty aluminum foil, place a handful of wood chips in the center, and nestle the fennel into the center. Cover with another sheet of foil and pinch together to create a sealed pouch. Poke 6 to 8 holes in the top and place directly on one side of the fire bed or directly on top of the burners on one side of a gas grill. (The pouch needs to be in direct contact with the heat source or it will not ignite.)

Wait until the chips and fennel begin to smoke. Lay the char fillets over the fire, with one side directly over the heat and the other side over the smoking pouch. After about 4 to 5 minutes, depending upon the thickness of the fish, turn over while also rotating the fillets 180 degrees. Grill for another 4 to 5 minutes. Remove and keep warm.

In the bowl of a food processor, puree the blueberries for about 1 minute. Strain through cheesecloth into a medium saucepan. Add the stock, liqueur, lemon juice, and thyme to the saucepan. Simmer over low to medium heat for 8 to 10 minutes or until reduced by half. Add the maple syrup and vinegar and simmer for 2 minutes.

Ladle the sauce onto 4 plates and lay a piece of fish on top of the sauce.

This is delicious served with lemon wedges, mashed celeriac with Yukon potatoes, and sautéed snap peas. Garnish it with strands of green fennel and lemon zest to offer a rich splash of colors—along with the blazing red of char and the deep blue of the sauce.

Wild Game Heart with Wild Oyster Mushrooms over Bow-Tie Pasta

(SERVES 4 AS AN APPETIZER)

1 pound venison heart (about 1 entire heart)

2 tablespoons butter

1/2 teaspoon canola oil

1 large white onion, finely chopped (about 1 1/2 cups)

6 garlic cloves, minced

3 ounces fresh oyster mushrooms, coarsely chopped

1 large tomato, chopped

1/4 cup scallion greens, finely chopped

1/2 cup dry red wine

1 can (12 ounces) tomato sauce

3 tablespoons black olives, pitted and sliced

1 tablespoon dried basil

1/2 tablespoon dried thyme

1 teaspoon cayenne

1 teaspoon salt

1 teaspoon coarsely ground peppercorns

1 pound bow-tie pasta

Grated cheese (optional)

Remove the veins from the heart. Cut the heart into 1-inch wide strips and then into 1/2-inch chunks. Set aside.

In a large cast iron skillet, melt the butter over medium-high heat. Add the onion, garlic, and mushrooms and sauté for 4 to 5 minutes, stirring occasionally. Push the vegetables to the edge of the pan and add the oil and heart meat. Sauté for 2 to 3 minutes. Add the tomato and scallions and sauté for 2 to 3 minutes, stirring occasionally. Add the wine and simmer for 1 minute. Add the tomato sauce, olives, basil, thyme, cayenne, salt, and pepper and simmer, partially covered, for 15 to 20 minutes.

Bring 4 quarts water to a boil in large saucepan. Add the pasta and simmer for 6 to 8 minutes. Drain and mix together with the heart sauce. Sprinkle grated cheese on top of each serving if you wish. Serve immediately.

Grilled Venison Satays

(SERVES 4)

4 12-inch wooden skewers, soaked in water

3 tablespoons toasted sesame oil or peanut oil

1/4 cup barbecue sauce

2 tablespoons maple syrup or honey

1/8 cup soy sauce

1/4 cup water

1/2 cup chunky peanut butter

1/2 tablespoon garlic, finely chopped

1 tablespoon Tabasco sauce

1 teaspoon ground cumin

1 teaspoon ground coriander

1/4 teaspoon cinnamon

1 tablespoon lemon juice

1 pound venison cut into 16 1 1/2-inch cubes

In the bowl of a food processor, add the oil, barbecue sauce, maple syrup or honey, soy sauce, water, peanut butter, garlic, Tabasco sauce, cumin, coriander, cinnamon, and lemon juice. Puree until smooth, about 1 minute. (If the mixture remains too thick, like peanut butter, add more water.) Transfer the mixture to an airtight container. Makes about 1 1/4 cups satay sauce.

In a shallow bowl, mix the venison cubes with half of the satay sauce. Cover and refrigerate for about 1 hour.

Preheat a charcoal grill. Remove the venison from the refrigerator. Skewer four pieces of venison onto each skewer, leaving space between each piece.

When the charcoals are gray and hot, lay the skewers on top of the grill. Turn after about 5 to 6 minutes and grill for another 5 to 6 minutes. Remove the skewers from the grill and slide the venison chunks off the skewers onto warmed plates. Serve immediately with warm, extra satay sauce for dipping.

Craig McNeil

Chef, Amsterdam Café
Kellyton, Alabama

In my years at *Gray's Sporting Journal*, I had read and heard about the elegant, classic Southern plantation hunts. Charley Dickey was perhaps the most eloquent on the subject:

"In the gray chill of winter mornings, long before the sunlight bounces through the longleaf pines and live oaks, there is a pervading sense of excitement in the barns and kennels. Handlers take quick swigs of misting coffee and banter with each other, the horses, the mules and dogs . . ."

So when chef Craig McNeil invited us to the Five Star Plantation, I was delighted at the opportunity to see a classic for the first time. Well, it sort of was my first. The only Southern bird hunt I done before had been a dove hunt gone inelegantly modern on us. It *was* North Carolina. And there was a handler, a kid who sported a transistor radio, which despite its being plugged into his ear, loudly and energetically announced every play of the Alabama football game. This assisted him, I'm sure, with moving the doves from their treetop roosts. There was food, although it came not from a great house but from the trunk of a great big sedan. And it was pretty obvious that no one at the meal even considered counting calories much less skipping the redeye gravy.

No doubt about it, I needed to revisit the whole concept of a Southern bird hunt. Five Star Plantation in Kellyton, Alabama, offered me the opportunity. Although time constraints limited the occasion and hunting possibilities, for me there was the next best thing: a tour and talk with the Plantation's chef, Craig McNeil.

For most of its history, Five Star Plantation was the property of Sidney Zollicoffer Mitchell, born in Dadeville, Alabama, in 1862. S. Z. was to become one of the nineteenth century's wealthiest men. A U.S. Naval Academy graduate, S. Z. was assigned to the U.S.S. Trenton and given the job of installing the first electric lighting system on an American Navy ship. His collaborator on the project was Thomas Edison. After two years of sea duty, S. Z. was discharged and hired by Edison. And by 1905, he'd created the Electric Bond & Share Company to fund small electric plants all over the world.

S. Z. returned to Alabama in 1927 as a guest at the dedication of the Alabama Power Company's newest dam, Ann Jordan Dam—named after Mitchell's grandmother—and it clearly was the place he wanted to come home to. He began purchasing the acreage near his boyhood home and by 1936 had acquired more than 5,000 acres, established the Ann Jordan Game Preserve, and built a lodge complete with carriage house, kennels, smokehouse, work shop, office, bunkhouse, and livestock facilities. It was a full working plantation—entirely wired and electrified, of course.

After S. Z. died in 1944, the plantation went to the University of Alabama. Then in 1994, William Ireland purchased it, decided to return it to its original elegance, and made it into a private hunting club, the Five Star Plantation. The lodge and outbuildings were totally renovated, kennels and stables reestablished, a helicopter pad built, and a program of conscientious wildlife management initiated to create habitat for bobwhite quail, pheasant, and chukar as well as turkey and deer. A 111-acre lake was stocked with bass and bream. And, of course, to guarantee the quality of the facility, capable and talented chefs were hired. The most recent was my host and guide.

Craig started his career as a fry cook, first at Long John Silver's and then at AVI Food Corporation, both in his hometown of Piqua, Ohio. He worked first as chef at the Piccolo Restaurant and The Red Bar in Grayton

Beach, Florida. Then he got a job as sous-chef at Bottchers in Auburn, Alabama, and later as pastry/lunch chef at Warehouse Bistro in Opelika. By the time Craig was twenty-four years old, he'd actually had a lot of culinary experience. So when he was offered the position at Five Star Plantation in August, 2000, it was an opportunity nearly impossible to pass on, especially if you list, as does Craig, your hobbies as bowhunting, shooting, camping, and fishing.

The dining room at the Plantation accommodates thirty-five diners, a manageable number for Craig, given his previous experience serving more than two hundred "covers" a night, but the demands of an exclusive clientele can impose a different kind of pressure on a chef. Craig recalls that on his third day on the job at Five Star, the governor of Alabama was visiting the Plantation for a squirrel hunt. Craig decided to make an especially perfect raspberry cheesecake pie for dessert. And it was quite perfect, until it slid off the serving platter onto the kitchen floor.

As Craig guided me around the Plantation, the pure elegance of a Southern hunting club wafted into my sensibilities: tasteful, comfy bedrooms; a large living room appointed with a stone hearth atop a warming fire and encircled with plump leather furniture; an efficient and scrubbed kitchen attached to a cheery dining hall; all introduced to us by a sunny front veranda. Outside the oaks swayed in the wind, giving way to vistas that pass through many miles of open and accommodating woods. The phrase "teeming with" pops to mind and promises good hunting.

In Craig's tour, there seemed to be a perfect balance of pride between fine and traditional Southern food and classic plantation hunting—from the classic walk-in smokehouse to the dog kennels with their champion English pointers. The stage is now set to review some of his culinary specialties: corn and crab chowder, fresh stone crab salad, braised pheasant Florentine with chive whipped potatoes and asparagus, banana cream cheesecake with crème anglaise, and blueberry bread pudding.

Craig is not only an able chef but a planner, an idea man, and very energetic when it comes to quality food. While at Five Star, he increased the smokehouse production and made signature Five Star Plantation smoked meats.

"I try to use only local farmers-market fruits and vegetables and have the seafood flown in fresh each day from Atlanta—my purveyors are everything," Craig said.

In 2001, Craig left Five Star Plantation to work at the Saugahatchee Country Club in Opelika, Alabama. Then he moved to Auburn, Alabama, to be closer to his home and wife—and now infant son. Currently, he is executive chef at the Amsterdam Café not far from Auburn University. But Craig talks of finding another hunting club and clearly feels—as do many chefs—that moving on is part of the learning process and part of being a good chef.

"I always want to learn," Craig said. "When I stop wanting to learn, that's the day I stop being a chef."

Rosemary Venison Stew

(SERVES 4 TO 6)

1 cup flour

2 tablespoons seasoned salt

2 tablespoons coarse black pepper

1 pound venison, cubed

1 pound unsalted butter

1 stalk celery, chopped

3 cups chopped carrots

2 tablespoons freshly chopped garlic

1 1/4 cups chopped yellow onion

2 large Idaho potatoes, peeled and chopped

1 cup chopped red cabbage

2 cups halved button mushrooms

2 tablespoons freshly minced rosemary

2 cups Cabernet Sauvignon

2 quarts beef stock

Salt

Pepper

In a mixing bowl, combine 1 cup of the flour, the salt, and pepper. Mix well to make seasoned flour. Dredge the venison in the flour.

In a medium stockpot, melt the butter over medium heat. Add the venison to the pot. Let the venison cook until it is golden brown.

When the venison has browned, add the celery, carrots, garlic, and onion. Allow this to cook for about 5 minutes and then add the potatoes, cabbage, mushrooms, and rosemary. Let this cook for about 3 to 5 minutes. Deglaze the mixture with the wine. With a wooden spoon, stir the ingredients well and allow the wine to simmer for several minutes. Then add the stock to the pot and let it simmer for 1 hour, or until the venison is tender. Stir the stew often to avoid scorching. Add salt and pepper to taste and enjoy!

This can also be done at the hunting camp or a campsite. All you need is a cast-iron pot and a good tripod stand with a little fire.

Braised Pheasant Florentine

(SERVES 4)

2 to 4 pheasant breasts
Salt
Pepper
1 tablespoon olive oil
3 garlic cloves, minced
1 cup white wine
Florentine Sauce (see recipe below)

Preheat the oven to 300 degrees. Lightly season both sides of the pheasant with salt and pepper. Heat a 10-inch, ovenproof sauté pan over medium heat. Add the oil, moving to coat the whole pan, and then the garlic. Add the pheasant and sauté until both sides are light brown. Add the wine to the pan and finish in the preheated oven until the pheasant is cooked to the temperature you like. Serve with Florentine Sauce (see recipe below).

■ ■ ■

Florentine Sauce

1 tablespoon butter
1 tablespoon chopped garlic
2 cups heavy cream
2 tablespoons chicken stock
1 cup chopped spinach

In a saucepan, heat the butter. Over medium heat, add the garlic to the hot butter and sauté until the garlic is golden brown. Add the cream and stock and simmer at a low heat. (Do not let the cream boil because this can cause the sauce to scorch.) Reduce the cream by half; it should coat the back of a spoon.

Once the sauce has been reduced, add the spinach, remove it from the heat and let it rest for 5 minutes. (This allows the spinach to release its flavor without overcooking.) After the spinach has turned bright green, your sauce is ready to serve.

Lemon-Grilled Cobia with Watercress Salad and Pineapple Vinaigrette

(SERVES 4)

1/4 cup olive oil
1 tablespoon ground coriander seeds
1 tablespoon kosher salt
1 tablespoon coarse black pepper
1 tablespoon grated lemon zest (yellow part only)
1 tablespoon freshly chopped parsley
Juice from two lemons
4 portions cobia fillet (6 ounces each)
Watercress Salad and Pineapple Vinaigrette (see recipe below)

In a medium bowl, combine the oil, coriander, salt, pepper, lemon zest, parsley, and lemon juice. Mix well with a whisk. Place the cobia fillets in the marinade for 6 hours.

Prepare the Watercress Salad and Pineapple Vinaigrette (see recipe below).

Fire up the grill for the cobia. Once the grill is hot, oil it, begin to cook the cobia, and be sure to eliminate the excess marinade on the fillets. (This will keep the grill from flaming up.) Grill the fish on each side for about 5 minutes, or until the fish is fully cooked.

Place the fish on the side of the greens, drizzle the vinaigrette over the salad, and enjoy!

This can also be accompanied with Mandarin oranges and toasted almonds.

· · ·

Watercress Salad and Pineapple Vinaigrette

1/3 cup white balsamic vinegar
2 tablespoons brown sugar
1 cup pineapple juice
1 tablespoon kosher salt
1/4 teaspoon white pepper
1/3 cup fresh chopped parsley
1/4 cup chopped golden pineapple
1/3 cup chopped pimentos
1 bunch watercress

In a mixing bowl, combine the oil, vinegar, sugar, pineapple juice, salt, pepper, pineapple, and pimentos. Mix well. (This vinaigrette is not emulsified, so it will separate. Mix it well just before you place it over the watercress and grilled cobia.)

Wash the watercress greens in cold water, and then place in an ice bath for about 2 minutes. (This ensures that the greens are clean and crispy.) Pull the greens out of the ice bath and shake them off to make sure there is no ice in the greens.

Joseph Messina

Owner, Adventure in Food, and Game Purveyor
Albany, New York

It was a cold and blustery afternoon, the forecast was for snow, but surely it was too early in November to snow in Vermont. Ed and I were driving to an inn just south of Lake Champlain in Bristol for the night, and, per usual, we were late. It was the annual wine and game dinner at the Inn at Baldwin Creek and Mary's Restaurant (see p. 98). We arrived just as snow began to fall and the buffalo and boar sausage was being set out for hors d'oeuvres. Handed a glass of Van Duzer sparkling wine as we passed through the common area, we bolted upstairs to our room, stashed the overnight bags, and returned to stand next to the blazing fireplace and drink our remaining half glass of bubbly.

We'd come, of course, to sample the great game dishes prepared by chef Doug Mack (see p. 98)—that was the task of the evening—and to interview him for this cookbook in the morning, post chaos of his preparing a game meal for seventy people.

As the room filled with guests, we stood close to the wall and, with journalistic reserve, observed the people. I remembered that Doug had also mentioned that his game purveyor would be at the dinner. Ah, another potential subject for my book, I thought, as I scanned the room, trying to guess who was likely the seller of game meats. No, they're too old, and not him, he's clearly a stockbroker from Manhattan, probably not with his wife. I solicited Ed's assistance in the game—matching a profession with a person's appearance—which we usually reserved for airports and boredom.

Suddenly the front door blew open, a gust of cold wind and tiny tornadoes of snowflakes entered first, followed by a very tall man. Stooping through the low threshold of the eighteenth century inn, the man was forced to remove his cowboy hat, revealing long, gray hair pulled taut into a ponytail. He wore a full length fur coat, which blew open as he entered, disclosing head-to-toe buckskin, trousers and shirt fringed on the outside seams. Ed and I looked at each other and simultaneously said, "Game purveyor."

It took till later in the evening to get introduced to Joe Messina, the owner of Adventure in Food, and till the next morning to interview him. But Joe's entrance was but a small preview to his exceptional devotion to wildness.

Although Joe was born in the Bronx, his family always had property in the Catskills, where they could retreat for weekends. When Joe was eight, they moved there to live full-time in Greenville, New York. Their home was an old resort, big enough to accommodate the hordes of family and friends who came to visit, many of them to hunt, and Sunday dinner often was for twenty people.

"The first time I hunted," Joe smirks, "I was a year old." As proof, he shows a photo of himself being pushed by his brother in a stroller, as they trail just behind their parents who were dressed in 1950s hunting garb and carrying shotguns.

Joe was young, too, when he made his first money as game purveyor, albeit illegally. Hunting parties from New York City came regularly in search of grouse and when Joe was eleven he recalls getting paid fifty cents for every grouse he shot and gave to the New Yorkers. At age fourteen, Joe started working at a local restaurant as a dishwasher, by sixteen, he was running the kitchen. Joe worked summers at what then was one of New York's top restaurants, Maplewood On the Lake, where the menu carried such exotic fare as whale steak and venison. Joe rose to the position of sous-chef, but then he decided a life of cooking wasn't for him.

Joe bounced around working construction, and later he helped his father who owned a string of Good Humor ice cream trucks. When Joe was thirty, he started a small gourmet foods business, "But I nearly starved trying to make it go," he recalls. So he made most of his money then by butchering the deer that hunters brought him and then selling the hides. He began to sell quail and rabbit wholesale. It was a scrappy existence. He remembers buying ten cases—three hundred pounds—of rabbit and not being able to sell it quickly enough, so it got freezer burn and he had to throw most of it out. But Joe kept at it and started his Tuesday Night Tastings, driving all over the Northeast to restaurants, cooking various game and letting restaurateurs and their guests sample the exotic meats.

In the early 1990s, Joe was invited to set up a concession at the Northeastern Wildlife Exposition. With volunteer student chefs from the Culinary Institute of America helping him prepare the foods, Messina sold his delicacies—alligator curls, rabbit kabobs, quail pâté—at his booth. He donated the proceeds to the CIA saying, "I wanted to do what I could for the next generation of chefs." Joe, with help from two of his restaurant friends, Carol Phillipi and Yono Purnomo, and the CIA students cooked at the Expo for five years, some years donating as much as $3,500 to the Culinary School. It was a big hit, but it took a tremendous amount of time. And by the late 1990s, as people traveled more and became knowledgeable about game and exotic meats and as it became more and more available in restaurants, there was less need to promote at the Expo.

"I'm not sure I could be considered a pioneer in the game food industry, but it certainly feels like it," Joe said. "One of the most difficult things for me to get is *real* elk. For many years most of the processors would switch large heavy red deer, label it as elk, and ship it. I lost a lot of business over the years not accepting switched meat. What is my most favorite game to eat? Probably caribou—it just dances on your tongue—but I'd have to say rabbit is the most fun to cook. It's so versatile."

As is predictable, Joe doesn't think much of beef or chicken. "It's just not that healthy," he said. "I prefer buffalo burger or quail that's not fed chemically-supplemented grains sprayed with pesticides."

A year passed since the night of talking to Joe at the Mary's Restaurant game dinner, but there had been vivid reminders of him over twelve months. I had a newspaper clipping of Joe with a giant—I mean giant, the size of a beach ball—puffball mushroom he'd found foraging. He sent pictures of his Crawford woodstove—he's very committed to woodstove cooking—and an article he wrote about various woods to use in the stove. And I called him with one last question for the book. I was curious about his opinion on the possible disparities between wild and farm-raised meats.

"I don't think there is much difference in how you cook wild versus farm-raised game, but there is a difference in how it tastes," Joe said. "The truly wild has more flavor, great character, and is just so intense! Gotta go now, my hunting buddies are here to go chase grouse."

Yes, the wild really do have great character and certainly are very, very intense.

Wild Game Trio

(SERVES 4)

Quail

8 quail
1/4 cup olive oil
6 stems fresh rosemary
Salt
Pepper
4 cups white wine
Chicken stock or other poultry stock (optional)

Sauté the quail in the oil until the skin is crisp on both sides. De-stem rosemary and sprinkle over quail. Add salt and pepper to taste. Sauté until the rosemary releases its aroma. Then add the wine and simmer covered 6 to 8 minutes until the quail is tender. Uncover and reduce the liquid until it thickens to a sauce. (If the sauce becomes too thick, add some stock.)

■ ■ ■

Bison

4 servings bison steak (4 ounces each)
Olive oil
Salt
Telicherry pepper

Coat the bison steaks with oil at least 3 hours before cooking. Sprinkle with salt and pepper. Grill very hot to no more than medium rare.

■ ■ ■

Pheasant

4 patties or links of pheasant sausage

Grill the sausage.

This trio is great served with Wild Rice Fritter Cakes (see page 139).

Field Greens of Romaine, Arugula, and Dandelion

(SERVES 6)

11 ounces romaine
1 1/2 ounces arugula
1 1/2 ounces dandelion
3 tablespoons olive oil
Sea salt
Pepper
1 garlic clove, minced
1/2 tablespoon lemon juice
1/2 tablespoon balsamic vinegar

Cut or tear the greens into fork-size pieces. Put the mixed greens in a large bowl and drizzle the oil over it. Add the salt, pepper, and garlic. Then drizzle the lemon juice and vinegar over the greens and mix thoroughly.

Wild Rice Fritter Cakes

(SERVES 4)

2 cups chicken broth
1/2 cup wild rice
1 egg, beaten
1/4 cup pine nuts, toasted
2–3 tablespoons flour
Salt
Pepper
4 tablespoons butter

In a saucepan, bring the broth to a boil. Add the rice and reduce the heat to a simmer. Once the rice is cooked, blend in the egg, flour, pine nuts, salt, and pepper. In a skillet, melt the butter. Fry serving-spoon-size portions of the batter in the butter and serve with the remaining butter drizzled over each fritter.

Sautéed Milkweed Pods
(SERVES 4)

2 quarts water
30 small milkweed pods, less than 4 inches in length
3 medium garlic cloves, finely chopped
2 tablespoons butter, melted
2 tablespoons olive oil
Salt
Pepper
Chile flakes (optional)
1 tablespoon balsamic vinegar

In a large pot, bring the water to a boil. Add the pods and return to a boil. Be certain all the pods are immersed thoroughly. Drain and reserve pods. In the same pot, sauté the garlic in the butter and oil. When the garlic begins to sizzle, add the blanched milkweed pods. Season with salt and pepper. (Add a few chile flakes if you like.) Sauté for approximately 8 to 10 minutes until the pods are cooked, stirring occasionally. Add the vinegar and cook for an additional 30 seconds.

Day Lily Fritters

(SERVES 4 AS AN APPETIZER)

12 day lily flowers
1 cup flour
Salt
Pepper
2 eggs
1/2 cup milk
1/2 cup grated Parmesan or Romano cheese
1 1/2 cups olive oil

Place the day lily flowers in a steamer and steam until wilted, about 2 to 4 minutes. Place in a strainer to drain. Place the flour in a bowl. Dredge the steamed flowers in flour. Season with salt and pepper.

In a bowl, beat the eggs and then combine with the milk and cheese.

Heat the oil in a medium-size frying pan. When the oil begins to smoke, dip the flowers into the egg mixture and place in the hot oil, turning when necessary to brown on all sides.

Cassoulet of Rabbit and Duck

(SERVES 4)

1 young fryer rabbit, cut up

2 duck legs and thighs, cut up, or duck breasts

Rendered duck fat or olive oil

1 1/4 pounds Basquaise sausage* or any spicy, hot pork sausage

1 medium onion, chopped

2 ounces pancetta

1/2 bulb garlic, chopped

Sea salt

Pepper

Sprinkle rosemary

Sprinkle sage

1 cup white wine

3 quarts poultry stock

1/2 cup dried porcini mushrooms, reconstituted

3 cups flageolet or cannellini beans, cooked

In a casserole dish, brown the duck and rabbit pieces in the rendered duck fat or olive oil and set aside. Brown the sausage in the same casserole dish and set aside. When the sausage is cooled, slice it. In the same casserole dish, sauté the onion until translucent, the pancetta until brown, and add the garlic. Add the sausage, rabbit and duck pieces back to the pan and season with salt, pepper, sage and rosemary. Pour the wine over the entire mixture. Add enough stock to cover all ingredients at least 3/4 of the way Add the mushrooms and their liquid and simmer for 2 hours. Add the cooked beans, bring to a boil, and reduce to simmer until flavors marry. Adjust seasoning and liquid if necessary.

Serve over a stale crusty bread.

* Available from Adventures in Food (www.adventureinfood.com)

Quail Braised in Wine Sauce

(SERVES 2)

4 semi-boneless quail

3 tablespoons olive oil or grapeseed oil

Salt

Pepper

Fresh herbs of your choice, such as rosemary, juniper, oregano, savory, sage, garlic, or thyme*

3/4 cup red or white wine

2 tablespoons butter

Dry the quail by patting with paper towel. Coat a heavy frying pan with oil and heat until it smokes. Place the quail in the pan over high heat. Fry until golden brown. Turn and fry on other side until golden brown. Reduce the heat to medium, add salt, pepper, and herbs of your choice. Simmer until the herbs release their flavors and aroma, about 2 or 3 minutes. Add the wine. Cover the pan and simmer over medium to low heat for 5 to 10 minutes until the quail are tender. Add the butter to thicken the sauce.

Do not use all of these herbs. Keep your choice simple.

Grilled Alligator Steaks

(SERVES 6)

2 pounds alligator tail steaks
1/4 cup olive oil
2 medium-size garlic cloves, finely chopped
2 tablespoons Italian parsley, finely chopped
Juice of 1/2 lemon
Hardwood fire for grilling

Marinate the alligator tail steaks in the oil, garlic, parsley, and lemon juice for a minimum of 1 hour. Three or four hours will add tenderness and flavor. Pour the marinade into a saucepan and heat, boiling it for a minute or two. Grill the alligator steaks over a hot wood fire very quickly, being certain not to overcook. Alligator is best cooked medium or rare. Dredge again in the marinade and serve.

Robert (Rob) Mondavi, Jr.

Director of Marketing, Robert Mondavi Winery
Napa Valley, California

"Food and wine are my life, hunting is my passion, and when they all come together, it's a rich and savory experience that is like nothing else for me."

This statement could ring a bit hollow or exaggerated had it not came from Rob Mondavi, oldest grandson and now director of marketing at the Robert Mondavi Winery in Napa Valley, California. Grandfather Robert Mondavi starting the winery in 1966, and with his sons Tim and Michael and daughter Marcia he built the successful wine business into a renowned force in the world of wine growing and producing and he created a family legacy as well. Along with Rob, several of his cousins work at the winery, and it is obvious and irrefutable that wine—coupled with food—is deeply embedded in the Mondavis' lives.

Rob Mondavi knows his vintner stuff. "When choosing a wine to go with fish or game—or any dish—begin selfishly by picking a wine that pleases you," Rob advised. "There are classic pairings of wine and food—a Pinot Noir with lamb, a 'cab' with steak—but start with personal taste and preferences and with what's going to bring pleasure. For example, I like a shiraz to go with the spicy richness of duck, but a '98 cab or a Pinot Noir can be just as satisfying. Choose whatever awakens your palate. Wine should not overwhelm but balance with the food. Wines, as well as foods, have different acidity levels, and attention needs to be paid here. Like when there is lemon in the recipe, remember it will bring out the fruitiness of the wine. Just enjoy the wine, don't be too much of a 'cork-sniffer.' They take it all way too seriously."

Of course being raised in a family of wine and food devotees does not *necessarily* also create a passion for hunting or an understanding of game cooking. I did have it on good authority—from Hot and Hot Fish Club chef Chris Hastings (page 59)—that Rob was the real thing. But I would reserve judgment—approaching Rob Mondavi's inclusion in this book with some caution—and wait for the telltale hunting conversations and recipes.

When I first spoke with Rob, he was living in Atlanta, Georgia. After graduating from Santa Clara University, he'd moved to Panama for a year to polish his Spanish language skills and learn something about international business. He came back to California in 1996 and started Napa Cigar Company, an importer of premium cigars from the Dominican Republic, Nicaragua and the Canary Islands. Then in 2000, he returned to Mondavi Winery to work in the Atlanta sales office. Rob's stories recalled times in Panama with his cousin Ramon, an avid hunter and restaurateur, hunting doves on coffee plantations and jump-shooting ducks in the wet and humid rice fields. Rob gave descriptions of his newfound Southern adventure, quail hunting. But his tales kept reaching back to California and when he was a kid.

"I remember watching wild turkeys feed in the 'cab' vineyard and hunting ducks with my grandfather, my mom's dad, on the vineyard's irrigation ponds or the Napa River, which borders the winery property," Rob said. "There was one time when my grandfather took me duck hunting in his Cadillac. He positioned me on one side of the pond and then drove the car around to the far side, pushing the ducks back at me, a true duck drive on several levels."

The Mondavi property was a dairy farm in 1915 and then rice fields; it certainly didn't lack for acreage or water. He started duck hunting with a bolt-action .410 on the ranch when he was twelve years old. Rob also had the benefit of growing up with ready access to the many California duck clubs. Ducks are still his favorite to hunt, so they must also be his favorite to eat, right?

Not exactly. Clearly a consummate Californian and outdoorsman, Rob's favorite fish or game meal is abalone seviche. Rob certainly had little reason to spend much time away from his home. He returned in 2003 to live in sight of the irrigation pond for Stag's Leap vineyard and where he can every morning drink his coffee and watch the mallards.

The man clearly likes his hunting. But fishing is part of Rob Mondavi's world, too. We had a long conversation about fly-fishing for bonefish and river fishing for salmon. We talked about the bamboo fly rod he first learned to fish with and the pros and cons of spey-casting. And he likes to free-dive for abalone.

"I always eat fish right away, very fresh, or else I give it away," Rob said. "I like sharing my fish."

So we take his passion for hunting and fishing and mix well with his food and wine heritage and knowledge. And what do we get? I waited for the recipes. Recipes, I find, reveal a great deal about their author. They are a kind of cryptic shorthand, a list of clues, which can provide dimension and insight into a person.

Rob's recipes were for duck, of course, and incorporated those ethnic culinary accents typical of California, Asian, and Latino. What I liked best about Rob Mondavi's recipes is they embodied two wine descriptors: unpretentious and honest. The recipes probably won't appeal to "cork-sniffers" but they surely are recipes that please Rob Mondavi—and probably many others as well. That's why they're included here. So do as Rob says, "Just enjoy!"

Duck Lettuce Wraps

(SERVES 3 TO 6 AS AN APPETIZER)

1–3 ducks, mallards, or pheasants
1 cup flour
1/2 teaspoon salt
1/2 teaspoon pepper
Vegetable or peanut oil
Sauce (see recipe below)
1 head iceberg lettuce, whole leaves separated
Sliced green onion
Chopped basil or mint

Breast the birds and cut into pieces near the size of a Hershey's Kiss, leaving the skin on, pat dry with paper towels. Set aside.

In a paper bag, mix the flour, salt, and pepper. Shake to mix. Then slowly drop the meat into the paper bag and shake until evenly coated.

Heat a large nonstick or very well seasoned cast iron pan on high. Coat the bottom of the pan with oil. Watch carefully; once the pan just begins to smoke, add the duck. Do not allow to stick to the pan and try to sear some of the sides for flavor. When the duck is almost finished cooking all the way through (just a few minutes), add about a quarter to a third of the Sauce (see recipe below) and allow to slightly reduce while coating the game. Remove from the stove and place immediately into a serving platter. Serve with the lettuce leaves. Garnish with a sprinkle of green onion and basil or mint.

■ ■ ■

Sauce

2 teaspoons sweet chilechili paste or 1 teaspoon honey and a small
  pinch of chilechili flakes
1 cup chopped cilantro
2 tablespoons rice vinegar, cider vinegar, or white wine vinegar.
Juice of 2 medium oranges
Juice of 1 lime
1 tablespoon soy sauce
1 tablespoon fresh ground ginger
1 teaspoon sesame oil

In a bowl, mix all of the ingredients together. Add the sesame oil
slowly, to taste. It is an intense flavor.

*Encourage your guests to eat the duck by placing a small amount of the sauce and meat
in the lettuce cups, taco-style. I suggest a Pinot Noir or a Fumé Blanc to accompany this dish.*

Great Tandoori Duck with Saffron Rice

(SERVES 4)

2 plucked ducks (larger birds such as a mallard or a chubby pintail are
  preferable)
Tandoori rub (either paste or powder)
Saffron rice, uncooked
Chicken broth or water
Mango or peach chutney

Breast the bird and cut away the thighs and legs together. Wash and
pat dry with paper towels. Over a flat container, dust the breast and
thighs and legs with the tandoori and coat well. (Tandoori spice is intense, so be cautious.) Allow to sit for a minimum of 1 hour or even
overnight. (I suggest 4 hours.)

Cook on an outdoor grill at medium-high to high heat. (You should
not be able to hold your hand over the grill for more than 3 seconds.)
Grill each side, allowing for the classic grill marks and cook to your desired level. For medium to slightly medium rare, cook hot and fast. After
the duck comes off the grill, allow the ducks to rest for at least 3 minutes
before serving.

Make the rice using half water and half chicken broth for added
flavor. Lay the grilled breast and one leg and thigh on a bed of rice.

Serve with a bit of mango or peach chutney.

*This dish can also be prepared inside in a cast iron skillet or under a hot broiler, but the
preferred method is on the grill. Because this dish is flavorful and spicy, I suggest a Zinfandel or a lively Cabernet Sauvignon.*

Marcel Mündel

Executive Chef, Le Château Montebello, Fairmont Château Laurier
Montebello, Quebec, Canada

For a long time now, I've prided myself on believing I knew about wild, what constitutes wild, and how to deal with it. I've actually made a whole career based on wildness, and I've spent a lot of time thinking and writing about it. And others have been convinced of my expertise, too, which presumably is why I was asked to be a judge at the 1996 National Wild Game Cooking Competition in Rice Lake, Wisconsin. The one fly in the soup was that heretofore my knowledge and experience were confined to creatures I hunted and to the culinary efforts of amateurs. But game is often about winging it, and I could and would. Plus perhaps this international event, with its many entrants of professional chefs, would serve to broaden the horizon on the provincial landscape of my wild cuisine.

The six finalists were all career chefs from US or Canadian restaurants and hotels. They set their creations before me for judgment: Cardomon-Cured Ostrich, Grilled Antelope Loin with Pumpkin-Banana Timale, Wild Turkey Ossobuco, Crusted Stuffed Bison with Balsamic Maple Wild Boar Bacon Glaze, Free-Range Partridge in Birch Bark, and African Lion Loin Medallions. Really. And most of it *really* wasn't very good. The birch bark "wrap" imparted a flavor to the partridge of, well, bark. The ossobuco was nicely prepared, but its large size betrayed it as a "wild" turkey impostor. And frankly lion loin, no matter how it's cooked, will always sound—and be—too tough for me.

I wondered what causes the sublime to be made into the ridiculous and complicated? Perhaps the chefs were, in some adolescent throwback mode, rebelling against restrictive game laws, which prohibit the taking of any wild game for the purpose of sale and limit commercial use of wild species to only those pen-raised. Barred, in their professional capacity, from cooking truly wild game perhaps they felt compelled to take their culinary skills to the extreme through the preparation of the not just wild but the wildly absurd. More likely, their stretch into the exotic was a symptom of boredom: Dazzle the diner through presentation of the weird, the unusual, and the never-before-tried; astound like a new starlet performing on a stage of culinary finesse. Well, it's better than pork chops.

But for all the "new" and ostentatious cooking present at the competition, I remained unmoved by the wild attempts of the chef competitors and didn't feel broadened in my knowledge of wild in the least. Instead, I became convinced that in game cookery there was little advantage to being a professionally-trained chef—in fact quite the contrary—and nothing out of a pen was worthy of the wild label.

Then in 1999, I met chef Marcel Mündel, who was at the time the executive chef at Le Château Montebello in Montebello, Quebec. Indeed Marcel was highly professional, yet his Roast Breast of Brôme Lake Duck with Spice Honey, Duck Leg Confit and Apples proved not only worthy, but superior. He made no attempt to razzle-dazzle; just simple—and to my mind simplicity is critical in game cooking—classic duck. So how is it that Marcel—unlike some of his hotel counterparts—felt no compunction to take his game cooking to the extreme? Marcel lived and cooked in one of Canada's great fish and game cornucopias an hour and a half drive west of Montreal and situated on the banks of the Ottawa River. The long-time Canadian Pacific hotel, Le Château Montebello, was built in 1930 and is believed to be the largest log structure in the world. A massive, wooden "castle" with some 210 rooms, indoor swimming pools and even a curling facility.

But the hotel's more fantastic feature is carved from the wildness. Connected to and part of the Hotel, down fifteen miles of dirt road, and past a manned gate is 65,000 acres of the once private and exclusive Seigniory Club.

The seventy-year-old sporting club—now owned like the hotel by Fairmont Hotels & Resorts (a company formed from the merging of Canadian Pacific Hotels & Resorts and the Fairmont Hotels) is one hundred square miles of lovely forested hills, trout streams, some seventy ponds and three deep-water lakes. Scattered reclusively about the old seigniory are thirteen electricity-less log cabins each outfitted with canoes and well-appointed with amenities such as built-in propane lanterns, hot water showers, hotel linens, and very functional kitchens. It's always nice to have a pleasant kitchen when on a hunting or fishing trip, but should you desire to stay out late hunting and prefer not to worry about meal preparation, one of the chefs from the Montebello will bring the makings to your cabin and prepare an excellent and very elegant dinner—or lunch or breakfast—for you.

Now called Kenauk, The Seigniory at Montebello, the reserve is teeming with wildlife, including small- and largemouth bass, pike, perch, walleye, black bears, coyotes, partridge, woodcock, deer, and moose. There's a small marina on the largest lake with motorboats for hire, and its hatchery stocks the lakes and streams with rainbow, brown, and brook trout. And for those not there during hunting season or desiring shooting practice there's a sporting clays course.

Rather astoundingly, the giant Château Montebello—the log "castle" with its six stone fireplaces and sixty-six-foot chimney rising through the center of the hotel lobby, cork-floored billiard room, two bars, and three great restaurants— was just the clubhouse for the Seigniory. It's as if Disney World and Yellowstone Park married and produced Kenauk. Such opulence in a wilderness setting surely dictates not only the best food but also the best game cooking.

Of course, as restricted in the commercial use of game as any chef, Marcel became a gatherer rather than a hunter of the season's bounty. He sought out local products, such as buffalo from nearby La Petite-Nation, trout from Kenauk's private hatchery, and, of course, duck from Brôme Lake.

Marcel oversaw a staff of forty who prepared an average of 1,200 meals a day. He was at the Montebello from 1995 to 2001, when the Fairmont Hotel & Resorts transferred him to another of their hotels, the Fairmont Château Laurier in Ottawa. Prior to that, he worked for Canadian Pacific at their Alberta hotel, Jasper Park Lodge, and at the Queen Elizabeth Hotel in Montreal.

Born in Alsace, the northeastern region of France bordering Germany, Marcel began his culinary training at the age of fourteen. He worked first in Strasbourg, Germany, and then in Switzerland, Norway, back to Germany, and back to Switzerland again—each country, each cuisine broadening his experience and influencing his cooking style. In 1981, Marcel immigrated to western Canada. He lived in Calgary for one year and then Edmonton, where he was briefly in partnership in his own restaurant. But in 1985, the Canadian Pacific Hotels recruited him. Interestingly, what is different with Marcel is he chose not to remain in the confines of a French culture and cuisine by emigrating to Quebec first but extended himself and his culinary repertoire to the Wild West. And although his later stint at the Queen Elizabeth Hotel proved a valuable stepping stone—he reached the position of executive sous-chef there—his next move to Montebello brought not only the executive chef title but a return to a rural setting much like the Alsatian town he grew up in.

Marcel once said, "At Le Château Montebello, we try to benefit from what the earth gives us and prepare dishes that reflect our nature. . . Our menus are an invitation to savor a world of authentic cuisine."

Pleasure in the genuine and uncontrived but innately spectacular, it expands my concept of wild yet is true to the philosophy of a great game cook.

Roast Breast of Brôme Lake Duck with Spiced Honey, Duck Leg Confit, and Apples

(SERVES 2)

- 1 Brôme Lake duck, breast left on the bone and legs removed
- 1 cup chicken stock
- 1 Granny Smith apple, quartered
- 2 tablespoons unsalted butter
- Spiced Honey (see recipe below)
- Olive oil

Preheat the oven to 350 degrees. In a skillet, slowly cook the duck legs in their own fat. Then set aside the legs to serve with the breast.

In a saucepan, blanche the duck breast for 5 minutes in the stock. In a skillet, sauté the apples in the butter. Spread the Spiced Honey (see recipe below) onto the duck breast. Sear the duck breast quickly in an ovenproof frying pan and then roast in the preheated oven for 10 to 15 minutes.

Serve with the light juice of duck enhanced with spiced honey and boiled potatoes.

■　■　■

Spiced Honey

(MAKES ENOUGH FOR SEVERAL DUCKS)

- 5 tablespoons crushed coriander
- 1 1/4 tablespoons pepper
- 2 tablespoons cumin
- 1 tablespoon savory
- 1 tablespoon nutmeg
- 1/2 teaspoon saffron
- 1 1/3 cup honey

In a bowl, combine all ingredients.

Ginger-Maple Marinated Trout Gravlax-Style
(SERVES 6 TO 8)

Salt

2 tablespoons grated fresh ginger

2 tablespoons *sève d'érable* (maple syrup)

Gingered Mayonnaise (see recipe below)

2 pounds rainbow trout fillets

1 cup maple sugar or brown sugar

1/4 cup coarse salt

In a non-reactive or glass pan, place half of the fish fillets, flesh side up.

In a bowl, mix together the maple sugar or brown sugar, salt, and ginger. Spread the mixture over the fish, then sprinkle with *sève d'érable*. Top with the remaining fish fillets, skin side up. Cover with plastic wrap and press down with a weight. Refrigerate for 24 hours.

To serve, scrape the excess marinade off of the fish. Slice thinly and arrange on chilled plates with a dollop of Gingered Mayonnaise (see recipe below).

• • •

Gingered Mayonnaise

2 tablespoons Dijon mustard

2 tablespoons maple syrup

2 cups mayonnaise

1 tablespoon grated fresh ginger

Fresh lemon juice

Salt

Freshly ground black pepper

In a small bowl, stir together the mustard, maple syrup, mayonnaise, and ginger. Season to taste with lemon juice, salt, and pepper. Refrigerate in a tightly covered container till needed. Makes about 2 cups. Can keep for several weeks.

Lea Nicholas-MacKenzie

Chef, New Sevogle Salmon Club
Miramichi, New Brunswick, Canada

E d and I had been fishing for Atlantic salmon and hunting woodcock at or near the Sevogle Salmon Club for many years. But the club had a new lodge and location on the Miramichi River. We opted for not forging the river in the dark and tried a shortcut instead. Then we got lost in the maze of back country logging roads. We were late and burst into the kitchen expecting to see Chantale Gratton (see page 38). Had I known she'd left the club? Now who would be cooking our dinner?

Greeted with a glass of wine by our dear friend and owner of the club, Steve Latner, we retired quickly to the screened porch on the river side of the house. We sat in the cold October air—with the porch heater adding warmth and a mellow glow of light—and listened to the river sliding along on its journey. Then a woman wearing a white jacket and blue baker's cap—the new headgear of choice in professional kitchens—came in, bearing an hors d'oeuvre of lightly grilled baby lamb ribs for us to gnaw on. Ah, yes, the chef. And once again that night I was surprised. Introduced as Lea MacKenzie, her Scottish last name didn't fit her Native American features. And her youth and full-time job in this wilderness camp kitchen didn't suggest a likelihood of it being a husband's name either. Yet this seemingly unlikely and incongruous detail about Lea was just the beginning. She would continue to go quite far beyond surprise, to reach the point of thoroughly astounding me—particularly in her culinary abilities.

"I've always eaten wild food," Lea said, "Moose meat and wild Atlantic salmon were a major part of what I grew up on. My father had a snare line, and we kept rabbits. And my whole family, but particularly my mother, had an interest and a concern about the quality of our food and diet. Long before it became popular, we were given yogurt for dessert in our school luncheons while the other kids got cookies."

Lea was raised in the Canadian provinces of Alberta and New Brunswick, and her Malecite ancestors had for generations hunted and fished the very land and river where we now so fleetingly did the same. Lea's great, great, great grandfather had been a renowned fishing guide for the British officers who came to occupy New Brunswick after the French and Indian Wars. Both her parents are university professors and encouraged her education. Lea graduated from the University of New Brunswick in 1991 with a Bachelor of Arts in French Language and Linguistics, the same year she married Rick MacKenzie. Lea continued her education, and in 1999, she earned her Master's in Leadership and Training from the Royal Roads University in Victoria, British Columbia.

In between Lea's undergraduate and graduate education and after, she worked at something else her parents encouraged, advocacy for Native Americans. Starting directly out of college, Lea worked with increasing responsibility in a wide variety of positions for Indian and Northern Affairs Canada. By 1998, she'd risen first to chief of staff, then to the political advisor to the national chief for the Assembly of Nations. But Lea's meteoric rise in the complex world of indigenous people and Canadian politics took its toll.

"It was dog-eat-dog, very rewarding, but stressful, and I just burnt out. I find cooking very therapeutic, being a chef has given me a much happier outlook," Lea confessed.

Lea had cooked for Steve Latner at the Sevogle Salmon Club one summer when she was still in college and loved it. So when her first career proved beyond demanding, she quit. She did still take consulting jobs; one for the International Work Group for Indigenous Affairs took her to Paris where her culinary interests were once again energized. Lea returned to cook at the Sevogle for a summer and then entered Le Cordon Bleu Ottawa Culinary

Arts Institute where she received her Grand Diploma in Cuisine and Pastry. Next, she worked at a chic, boutique hotel in Ottawa, Arc the Hotel, with a small twenty-two-seat restaurant. She was there for a year under the tutelage of a talented Mexican chef, René Rodriguez. And then she went back to work at the Sevogle Salmon Club.

"I had learned in cooking school that the Native way—to use every bit of the animal when you cook—was also the French way," Lea said. "And I was encouraged, as were my classmates, to blend personal culinary history and culture with the skills learned at the school. So I cooked braised moose for my final exam. Game in particular has a special, unique and untampered-with flavor. The meat dictates, not you, and it is humbling to cook. At the Sevogle, I cook in an environment where quality of ingredients is important, so I can get the best and I appreciate that. But I do miss my husband when I'm up here. [Rick MacKenzie works in Ottawa for the British High Commission.] I like spending time with him and our German shorthairs, hunting and fishing."

At our meal the following evening, Lea stood patiently tableside. It had been a hard day of hunting for us, rainy and cold and few birds. We'd come back from the hunt to beautiful local Malpec oysters, a glass or two of champagne, a hot shower, and then dinner from Lea. In the exquisite, austere style of Japan, Lea presented each of us with a black lacquer tray carrying a trinity of perfectly prepared game. She spoke quietly, reverently, of what she'd placed before us: Duck Confit Spring Rolls with Maple Soy Dipping Sauce, Woodcock Sausages with Rhubarb-Port Syrup and Pancetta-Wrapped Grouse with Wild Grape Sauce. The meal moved on through salad and cheeses and dessert, but the magnificence of the main course was impossible to forget. Of course, the culinary philosophy deployed was yin and yang, obviously so in flavors and appearance, but it went beyond to a higher state: the sensuality of oysters and champagne, the power of meat from birds brought to the table by your own hand. Or is it the clear, earthy taste of the birds that are sensual and the aphrodisiac of the oysters that have the power? I've only seen this kind of ultimate yin and yang induced with seafood and game—and then always prepared by a master.

Lea clearly has a gift; a gift which is augmented by Steve Latner's good sense of how to be a patron of the culinary art and his own love and superb understanding of food and wine. We felt honored to be involved in the product of this great partnership, but we knew it would not last. The goal of a talented chef is not just sustenance, but to have a deeper effect and to surprise the audience—always surprise. Lea did that. And then she moved on. Now, perhaps unsurprisingly, she is the sous-chef for the Prime Minister of Canada.

Marsala Braised Moose and Pearl Barley Risotto

(SERVES 6 TO 10)

2 pounds moose blade roast, deboned and cubed (reserve bones and trimmings for Sauce)

Canola oil

1 medium carrot, peeled and chopped

1 small onion, peeled and chopped

1/2 stalk celery, chopped

1 tablespoon tomato paste

1/3 cup Marsala

1 cup veal stock

1 piece bouquet garni (thyme, parsley stems, and bay leaf tied with kitchen string)

4 tablespoons butter

Pepper

2 tablespoons olive oil

1/2 small onion, minced

1 cup pearl barley

1/4 cup Madeira

3–4 cups veal stock

1/4 cup Parmesan cheese, grated

1/4 cup chives, chopped

Salt

White pepper

Preheat the oven to 350 degrees. In a heavy pan, sear the moose cubes in the canola oil. While browning, season meat with salt and pepper. Once browned, remove the meat from the pan, slightly degrease the pan and sweat the carrot, onion, and celery in the same pan. (To sweat means cooking vegetables in a small amount of fat over low heat.) Add the tomato paste, return the moose to the pan, and deglaze with the Marsala. Reduce the Marsala and add the veal stock and the bouquet garni. Bring the liquid to a simmer, cover the pan, and braise the moose in the preheated oven for 2 hours or until the meat is tender and falling apart. Meanwhile, start the Sauce (see recipe below) and prepare the Garnish (see recipe below).

When moose is braised, remove from braising liquid and shred coarsely. Remove the carrot, onion, and celery and reserve. Strain the braising liquid through a fine mesh sieve and continue to skim impurities and reduce. Strain the liquid again and continue to skim and reduce. Reheat and glaze the carrots, celery and onions in a separate pan with butter, salt, and a few drops of water. Once the sauce is the desired consistency, check and adjust the seasonings, then add cubes of butter gradually while swirling the pot to emulsify. (Do not allow sauce to boil after adding butter or it will break.) You'll use this mirepoix in the Sauce.

To make the risotto, sweat the minced onions in olive oil, then add the barley and stir to coat each grain with oil. Add the Madeira and stir constantly until the liquid is almost gone. Add the stock gradually, allowing the liquid to simmer, stirring constantly between each addition, and waiting until liquid is almost gone before adding more. When the barley is cooked to a chewy consistency, add the shredded moose and Parmesan cheese. When ready to serve, stir in the chives.

To serve, spoon the moose risotto onto plates, add Sauce around the risotto and garnish with three carrots and an onion, chive tips and cut chives.

Sauce

Moose bones (trimmings reserved from moose)
Canola oil
1/3 cup mirepoix (see description above p. 162)
1/4 cup Marsala
2 cups veal stock
1 piece bouquet garni
Butter to finish sauce, about 4 tablespoons
Salt
Pepper to taste

In a skillet, sear the moose bones and trimmings in oil. Remove bones and trimmings and add the mirepoix and Madeira. Reduce and add the stock and bouquet garni. Simmer and skim impurities constantly. Season with pepper to taste.

. . .

Garnish

Baby carrots, peeled
Salt
Green onions, trimmed
Chives

Cook the carrots in boiling, salted water until just tender but still firm, and refresh in ice water. Drain and reserve. Blanch the green onions in boiling water. Refresh, drain and reserve. Cut the chives on an angle, reserving the chive tips.

Woodcock Sausages with Rhubarb-Port Syrup

(MAKES ABOUT 12 TO 16 SAUSAGES)

12 ounces boneless and skinless woodcock breasts, ground or finely
    chopped (about 6 breasts)

12 ounces ground pork

3 tablespoons duck fat

3 tablespoons dried cherries, coarsely chopped

3 tablespoons ruby port

2 teaspoons nutmeg

Salt

White pepper

Rhubarb-Port Syrup (see recipe below)

Baby arugula leaves (for garnish)

Extra virgin olive oil

Fleur de sel

In a bowl, mix the woodcock, pork, and duck fat with the dried cherries, port, and nutmeg and salt and pepper to taste. Check the seasonings by frying a little of the mixture. Adjust the seasonings if necessary. Place 2 tablespoons of the mixture on a piece of plastic wrap and roll to form sausages approximately 3 inches in length. Secure the ends with kitchen twine and reserve. Bring a large pot of water to a rolling boil, add the still-wrapped sausages, and poach 5 minutes, until just cooked through. Remove the sausages from the water and cool, then store in a tightly wrapped container until ready to use (Note: These are best made a day or two ahead.)

Prepare the Rhubarb-Port Syrup (see recipe below).

In a bowl, toss the arugula leaves in the oil and sprinkle with the fleur de sel. Set aside.

Remove the plastic wrap from the sausages and cook in a skillet over medium heat until browned and heated through. Drizzle with the Rhubarb-Port Syrup and garnish with the arugula.

. . .

Rhubarb-Port Syrup

1/2 cup ruby port
1/2 cup sugar
3 cups rhubarb, chopped
1 tablespoon pink peppercorns

In a saucepan, combine the port and sugar and simmer until the sugar dissolves. Add the rhubarb and cook until very soft, approximately 20 minutes. Strain through a fine mesh sieve and pour into a clean saucepan. Reduce slowly to a syrup, skimming froth as needed, about 10 minutes. Add the peppercorns and reserve at room temperature.

Pancetta Wrapped Grouse with Wild Grape Sauce

(SERVES 4)

2 grouse, skinned and deboned, breasts set aside and bones reserved
   for Wild Grape Sauce
16 slices pancetta, very thinly sliced
Salt
White pepper
1 teaspoon duck fat*
Wild Grape Sauce (see recipe below)
Baby watercress (for garnish)

Pound the grouse breasts between 2 pieces of plastic wrap to an even
thickness. On a work surface, slightly overlap 4 slices of pancetta, to
form a square, and set a grouse breast on top. Season with salt and pepper. Roll the pancetta and grouse up and secure at 1-inch intervals with
kitchen twine. Repeat with the remaining pancetta and grouse. Reserve.

Preheat the oven to 350 degrees. In an ovenproof skillet, heat the
duck fat over medium heat. Sear the grouse breasts on all sides, then put
the skillet into the preheated oven for 5 to 10 minutes until grouse is
cooked through. Remove the grouse from the oven, remove the twine,
and allow the breasts to rest for a few minutes. Slice the grouse on the diagonal, set on a pool of sauce, and garnish with watercress.

*Duck fat adds great flavor although it can be very salty. Taste the fat before using, and
if it is salty use a low-sodium chicken broth in place of the chicken stock in this recipe. Or if
duck fat is hard to come by, substitute canola, olive, or peanut oil.*

Wild Grape Sauce

1/2 cup water
2 cups wild grapes or Concord grapes
1 1/2 tablespoons sugar
Reserved grouse bones
1 tablespoon duck fat*
1 teaspoon garlic, finely minced
1 tablespoon shallots, finely minced
3 cups chicken stock or low-sodium chicken broth
1 tablespoon maple syrup

Place the water and sugar in a saucepan and simmer until the sugar dissolves. Add the grapes and cook slowly until soft, approximately 20 minutes. Strain through a fine mesh sieve and discard the solids. Set aside 1/4 cup of grape juice for the sauce, reserving the remainder for another use.

Meanwhile, brown the bones in the duck fat in a medium saucepan. Once brown, add the garlic and shallots and caramelize. Add the stock and bring to a simmer. Skimming occasionally, reduce the sauce slowly until it coats the back of a spoon. Strain through a fine mesh sieve into a clean saucepan, add the reserved 1/4 cup grape juice and the maple syrup. Simmer and reduce to desired consistency. Taste and adjust seasonings. Set aside, keeping warm.

Duck Confit Spring Rolls with Maple Soy Dipping Sauce

(MAKES 8)

Duck Confit

1 teaspoon coriander seeds
1 tablespoon white peppercorns
1 piece star anise
1 teaspoon Szechwan peppercorns
1 tablespoon turbinado sugar or raw sugar
3 tablespoons coarse salt
1/2 teaspoon nutmeg
4 wild duck legs with thighs
2 cloves garlic, halved
4 sprigs fresh thyme
4 cups duck fat

In a small skillet over medium heat, lightly toast the coriander seeds, white peppercorns, star anise, and Szechwan peppercorns. When fragrant, grind in a spice grinder and mix with the sugar, salt, and nutmeg. Rub the duck legs with the garlic, and then the salt mixture. Place in a glass container with the thyme and garlic and cover tightly with plastic wrap. Let sit in refrigerator overnight.

The next day, preheat the oven to 300 degrees. Rinse the duck legs and pat dry with a paper towel. In a heavy ovenproof pot, melt the duck fat and add the thyme and garlic from the glass overnight container.

Completely submerge the duck legs in fat, cover, and bake in the pre-heated oven until the meat is very tender and falling from bones (about 2 to 3 hours). Remove the duck legs from the fat and cool. Once cool, shred the meat coarsely. Strain and reserve the duck fat for another use.

. . .

Spring Rolls

1 tablespoon coriander seeds, coarsely chopped
2 tablespoons shallots, chopped
1 tablespoon duck fat
Reserved duck confit, shredded (about 1 cup) (see recipe above)
1/4 cup fresh orange juice
1 tablespoon tamari soy sauce
1/4 cup fresh coriander, coarsely chopped
8 small spring roll wrappers (about 4-by-4-inches square)
1 egg, beaten with a few drops warm water
Peanut oil
Baby purple shiso leaves or purple basil for garnish
Maple Soy Dipping Sauce (see recipe below)

In a large skillet, sauté the shallots and coriander seeds in the duck fat. Add the duck confit, then deglaze the skillet with the orange juice and cook until very little liquid remains. Add the soy sauce and remove from heat. Cool completely, then fold in the fresh coriander.

Roll spring rolls using approximately 1 1/2 tablespoons of duck mixture per spring roll wrapper, sealing with the egg mixture. Reserve.

Heat the oil to 350 degrees, then add the spring rolls and deep fry for 2 to 3 minutes, or until golden brown. Garnish with purple shiso leaves or purple basil and serve with Maple Soy Dipping Sauce (see recipe below).

■ ■ ■

Maple Soy Dipping Sauce

1 tablespoon grapeseed oil
2 tablespoons fresh ginger, finely minced
2 tablespoons shallots, finely minced
2 cloves garlic, finely minced
Pinch chile flakes
1/4 cup mirin rice wine
1/4 cup tamari soy sauce
2 tablespoons maple syrup
1 teaspoon coriander seeds

Heat the oil in a medium skillet, then add the ginger and shallots, cooking slowly until the shallots are translucent (do not brown). Add the garlic and chile flakes and cook for another minute, then add the mirin, soy sauce and maple syrup. Bring just to a boil and immediately remove from heat and pour into serving bowl.

In a small dry skillet, toast the coriander seeds lightly, then crush with the side of a knife and stir into dipping sauce. Reserve at room temperature.

Wayne Nish

Chef and Co-owner, March
New York, New York

"I think game and vegetarian cooking are a lot alike," Wayne Nish said as we sat at a damasked table in his New York city restaurant, March. The remark inspired a flash of confusion as I recalled the scene of my most recent game dinner: A large platter was abundantly piled with lightly grilled woodcock each encrusted with juniper berries and beach plum jelly, oozing with an au jus tinged with blood. And the dinner guests, abandoning tableware, were voraciously gnawing on the burgundy-colored and very rare little carcasses. I squinted and wondered how that scene was in any way comparable to the often minimalist and always bloodless meal of a vegetarian?

"Both cooking styles are long on philosophy and short on applied skill," Wayne explained.

There was truth in his proclamation, albeit a somewhat eccentric view of the two cuisines, but then Chef Nish's relationship with food has often been eccentric.

Wayne's first career interests were not culinary. He studied journalism and architecture in college and abandoned both to venture into the printing business. But in 1983 at the age of thirty-two and after a honeymoon in Europe, Wayne decided to become a chef and entered the New York Restaurant School. Only a slightly impetuous move, he had actually been employed as a fraternity house cook during his college years and the experience—although lacking in food finery—taught something at least of the routine. And later, while working a four-day work week at his New York City printing business, Wayne spent his free time perusing the food displays at Balducci's, rambling through Chinatown's grocery stores, teaching himself to make veal stock, and, in general, reveling in the pleasures of cooking.

Wayne grew up in Queens, the son of a Norwegian-Japanese father and Italian mother. So his heritage and the neighborhood provided culinary background for his instinctual ability, and in addition gave him the basis for innovation. First, Wayne's skills and technique were practiced as an apprentice at the famed Quilted Giraffe. Next, there was a brief stint as a private chef followed by acceptance of the executive chef position at La Columbe d'Or. There Wayne received a three-star review from the *New York Times,* and he was suddenly catapulted into chef stardom.

In 1990, Wayne and partner Joe Scalice opened March and Wayne's New American cuisine continued to win him many more accolades.

"The menus are works in progress as I continue to experiment with new ingredients and multi-ethnic and multi-cultural influences," Wayne said. "I want to solidify my own personal imprint on New American cuisine, which is, by my definition, global in scope."

Surely it was this quest of Wayne's to experiment with new ingredients and define an American cuisine that would bring him ultimately to game cooking—and to game procurement.

Wayne didn't grow up hunting but with the impetus of obtaining unusual ingredients and using fine English shotguns to do so, he would quickly become a devotee. Yet he entered the world of game cooking with some skepticism.

"I must admit the whole notion of 'camp meat' [not aged and perhaps not handled properly] is frightening . . .that, and the concept to many hunters that the *use* of the animal is tertiary," Wayne said. "But a good cook must learn everything about what there is to cook."

When I first met Wayne, he was fully immersed in applying his art to game cookery. He'd just returned from Newfoundland, bringing back the caribou he'd shot, bone-in and still awaiting completion of the aging process. Simultaneously Wayne was designing the menu and making preparations for cooking at the annual shoot of the Pheasant Ridge Preserve in upstate New York, and he was spending his mornings woodcock hunting. Wayne knew the wily woodcock's reputation as food—dark, distinctive meat, earthy and pungent and slight—he wanted to try it, if he could ever shoot enough. Luckily, I happened to have a very limited supply left from my annual woodcock hunt.

The scene was set in the kitchen of March. It was classic restaurant kitchen, classic New York. In the lower levels of a Sutton Place brownstone, burners blazing, a gargantuan stockpot percolating in the corner, and coveys of pans hanging overhead; I brought forth from my insulated game bag four plucked and cleaned woodcock. We discussed.

"Rare is better with these birds," I said.

Wayne smiled, listened, and began to move about the kitchen, already intent on what he was conjuring up.

"And how are the legs? Tough?" he asked.

Actually I didn't usually bother with the legs, so little and tough, so much effort. But Wayne was intent and began to chop the legs off and throw them into a small pot along with chicken stock, shallots, garlic, coriander seed, a fresh blade of mace (just off the nutmeg seed), fresh thyme, Brittany sea salt, and peppercorns. During the braising, we would retire upstairs to the dining room to talk food and delve into some of Wayne's cooking theorems: Strive to utilize as much of the critter as possible; everything on the plate should be edible; and serve small portions in multiple courses because after three or four bites "we've visited" that taste and the rest is uneventful. Presently I departed, leaving Wayne to prepare dinner.

I returned with Ed for dinner, and we embarked on our culinary excursion with one of Wayne's signature dishes: Three tiny little crêpes, one filled with lobster and black truffles, a second with foie gras and smoked salmon, and a third with or osetra caviar and crème fraîche, each tied into a pouch-shaped morsel with a zucchini-skin ribbon. That was just the beginning. What was to follow were some fourteen different slices of sheer heaven: sliced foie gras de canard with Indian spices, crisp black figs, and green tomato marmalade; sashimi of yellowfin tuna with olive oil and white soy sauce; Prince Edward Island lobster in muscat de beaumes de venise sauce; a sweetbread ravioli with parsnip and cumin in herbal broth; a Midori and honeydew melon, and more. Each was perfectly matched with a wine, sherry, sake, or champagne. To describe the meal as "unparalleled" or "spectacular" is surely a gross understatement.

And the woodcock? Yes, it was perfectly placed amongst the other gourmet treats (as was the bit of Wayne's caribou which he cooked for us) and indeed could be designated the *pièce de résistance* for me. The little braised legs were so exquisitely prepared that the tender, succulent meat literally fell from the bone. Wayne was right not to disregard any part of the bird. The breasts, too, were wonderful.

As I sat there eating the woodcock I squinted, again. What was that comparison? Philosophy? Skill? On that you are incorrect, Wayne Nish. There simply are no comparisons between woodcock and rutabagas, not with your skill and your philosophy.

The Perfect Venison Burger

(SERVES 4)

With venison, the first requirement is proper handling of the meat. It must be aged for at least a week and never frozen before it's ground. (Freezing meat is an extreme preserving technique and can cause as much as a 30 percent loss of moisture—blood and other flavor elements—in the meat.) Also, it's critical to start with the gold standard for preparing a great beef burger, which is to use 20 percent beef fat with the chuck. If you do these two things, there will be enough flavor in the meat so virtually nothing else needs be added to make the perfect venison burger. If you need to add onions or a lot of spices, you're really making meat loaf, not a burger.

1 pound venison shoulder with fat and sinew removed, cut into 1- to 1 1/2-inch cubes
3 ounces beef fat
Kosher or good quality sea salt
Tomato slices
Lettuce
4 rolls

Using the large size disk (#2) feed the venison cubes, along with pieces of the beef fat into the meat grinder. Grind only once.

Heat a charcoal fire or grill. Divide the meat into fourths and form into patties. Sprinkle the patties with kosher salt and grill over a charcoal fire until medium rare. Serve on rolls with tomato slices and lettuce.

March Woodcock in Puff Pastry

(SERVES 4 AS AN ENTRÉE)

8 North American, or 4 European woodcock, plucked and cleaned
  (reserve the entrails, heart and liver)

1/4 cup cognac

Olive oil

Salt

Pepper

8 baked puff pastry shells

Woodcock Legs (see recipe below)

Sauce (see recipe below)

1 tablespoon unsalted butter

4 ounces wild watercress (preferably from a stream near where the birds
  were taken), or arugula

A day in advance of serving, remove the entrails of each bird (hearts
and livers included), and discard the gizzard, which may contain sand.
Chop the entrails finely and place them in a small ceramic or stainless
steel bowl. Stir in the cognac and cover tightly with plastic wrap. Reserve,
refrigerated, for the Sauce (see recipe below).

Cut off the woodcock legs and thighs, each in one piece, with a small
paring knife. Reserve for the Woodcock Legs (see recipe below).

Cutting along the top of each breastbone, cut off each breast half,
cover tightly with plastic wrap and refrigerate until ready to use. Save the
carcasses for the Game Stock (see recipe below).

Preheat a small sauté pan. Add the oil. Lightly salt and pepper the breasts and place them skin side down in the pan. Sauté the breasts for about 1 minute, turn and cook for another 30 seconds. Remove from the pan and drain. Carve each breast half into 4 slices. Add the Woodcock Legs (see recipe below) to the same pan skin side down and brown lightly. Turn and brown on the other side. Remove from the pan and drain. Wipe out the pan with a paper towel and add the butter. When melted, add the watercress over high heat to wilt rapidly. Remove from the pan immediately, and drain.

On each of 4 warm dinner plates, place 2 puff pastry shells. Place an equal amount of wilted watercress inside each shell. Spoon an equal amount of Sauce (see recipe below) on top of each one. Arrange 2 woodcock legs standing up towards the back inside each pastry shell, and tuck 2 sliced breast halves into each pastry shell.

· · ·

Game Stock

Carcasses
2 tablespoons olive oil
2 shallots, peeled and sliced
5 garlic cloves, peeled and lightly crushed
1 tablespoon black peppercorns
1 tablespoon coriander seeds
4 bay leaves
2 sprigs fresh thyme
1 bunch flat leafed parsley
4 cups chicken stock

Chop the carcasses into 1-inch pieces, or smaller. Preheat a 6-quart saucepan, add the oil, shallots, garlic, peppercorns, coriander seeds, bay leaves, thyme, parsley, and the chopped carcasses. Cook over low heat for 3 minutes. Add the stock. Simmer for 3 hours. Let cool, strain the solids out, and reduce to 1 cup. Reserve for the Sauce (see recipe below).

■ ■ ■

Woodcock Legs

2 tablespoons sea salt
Woodcock legs
2 cups rendered duck fat *
2 shallots, peeled and sliced
5 garlic cloves, peeled and lightly crushed
1 tablespoon black peppercorns
1 tablespoon coriander seeds
4 bay leaves
2 sprigs fresh thyme
1 bunch flat leafed parsley

Sprinkle the sea salt over the woodcock legs. In a 6-quart saucepan, add the duck fat, shallots, garlic, peppercorns, coriander seeds, bay leaves, thyme, parsley, sea salt, and the woodcock legs and thighs. Simmer for 3 hours, or until the legs are tender to the touch. Let cool in the fat to room temperature. Drain the legs on paper towels and reserve until ready to use. Discard the fat and the solids.

■ ■ ■

Sauce

2 tablespoons unsalted butter
1 shallot, peeled and finely chopped
1 garlic clove peeled and finely chopped
1 teaspoon sea salt
Reserved 1 cup reduced Game Stock (see recipe above)
Reserved entrails in cognac

Melt the butter in a small saucepan, and add the shallot, garlic, and salt. Cook over a low heat for 3 minutes, or until translucent and soft. Add the stock and bring to a simmer. Gently stir in the entrails. Taste to correct for seasoning and set aside in a warm place.

Duck fat is available from D'Artagnan (see page 15). Alternatives to duck fat are chicken fat, pork fat, beef fat, or peanut or corn oil.

Fricasse of Game Birds with Winter Vegetables and Chestnuts

(SERVES 4)

1 red bell pepper

1 cup 1/2-inch cubes peeled acorn squash

1 cup 1/2-inch cubes peeled Yukon gold potatoes

1 cup green beans, cut into 1-inch lengths

1 tablespoon plus 1/2 cup olive oil

4 quail or 2 partridge, quartered and backs removed

Salt

Pepper

1 cup chopped portobello mushrooms (about 2 ounces)

8 cups coarsely chopped greens (such as spinach, arugula, bok choy, kale, or Swiss chard)

24 vacuum-packed chestnuts*

1 cup cherry tomatoes, halved

2 cups chicken stock or canned low-sodium broth

2 tablespoons chopped fresh thyme

2 tablespoons chopped fresh basil

Char the bell pepper over a gas flame or under the broiler until it is blackened on all sides. Seal in a paper bag and let stand for 10 minutes. When it is cool, peel, seed, and chop the bell pepper.

Cook the squash and potatoes in a large pot of boiling water for 2 minutes. Add the green beans and cook 1 minute. Drain. Rinse under cold water. Drain again. (The roasted pepper and squash and potato mixture can be made a day before.)

Heat 1 tablespoon of the oil in a heavy large Dutch oven over medium-high heat. Season the game birds with salt and pepper. Working in batches, add the game birds to the Dutch oven and cook until brown on all sides and almost cooked through, turning frequently, about 10 minutes per batch. Transfer the game birds to a platter. Add the mushrooms to the Dutch oven and sauté for 1 minute. Stir in roasted bell pepper, squash and potato mixture, greens, chestnuts, and tomatoes. Top with the game bird pieces. Pour the stock and the remaining 1/2 cup of oil into the Dutch oven. Cover and simmer until the game birds are cooked through, stirring occasionally, about 15 minutes.

Transfer the game birds to a warm platter. Stir in 1 tablespoon each of thyme and basil into the vegetable mixture and season to taste with salt and pepper. Divide the mixture on to 4 plates and top with the game bird pieces. Sprinkle with the remaining thyme and basil.

Vacuum packed chestnuts are sold in specialty food stores or specialty sections of good supermarkets.

Grilled Quail and Seared Squab with Persimmon Chutney

(SERVES 6)

Squab

1/2 cup unsalted, clarified butter

3 squabs, breasts removed and boned, legs removed and leg knuckles trimmed and carcasses chopped

3 cups water

1/4 cup coriander seeds

1 tablespoon black peppercorns

3 bay leaves

2 shallots, peeled and minced

1 tablespoon vegetable oil

Sea salt

Pepper

In a large saucepan, heat the butter over medium-high heat. Add the squab legs and carcasses and sauté until well browned Add the water, coriander seeds, black peppercorns, bay leaves, and shallots. Raise the heat and bring to a boil. Reduce the heat, cover with parchment paper, and simmer for 1 1/2 hours. Remove from the heat and transfer the squab legs to a paper towel–lined plate to drain and set aside.

In a large sauté pan, heat the oil over medium heat. Season the squab breast and legs, place in the pan and sear until well browned and cooked to desired doneness. Remove from the heat and set aside, keeping warm.

· · ·

Quail

3 quail
Vegetable oil
Salt
Pepper
Radish sprouts (for garnish)

For the quail, prepare a hot grill. Brush the quail with oil, season with salt and pepper, and place on the grill, cooking on all sides to desired doneness. Remove from the grill, slice into quarters, remove the bones from the breasts, and set aside, keeping warm.

· · ·

Persimmon Chutney

2 tablespoons vegetable oil
1/2 cup garam masala*
5 unripe persimmons, peeled, stemmed, and chopped
2 tablespoons brown sugar cane*
5 garlic cloves, peeled and minced
1 Thai chili pepper, split
1 plum tomato roasted, peeled, seeded, and chopped
1 cup water
Sea salt
Pepper

In a medium saucepan, heat the oil over low heat. Add the garam masala until the seeds begin to pop and the cinnamon begins to unfurl. Remove from the heat, strain the oil into a second medium saucepan, and discard the garam masala. Place the seasoned oil over medium heat and add the persimmons, sugar, garlic, chili pepper, tomato and water. Cover and bring to a boil. Reduce the heat and simmer for 30 minutes. Season with salt and pepper, remove from the heat, and set aside, keeping warm.

. . .

To Serve

Slice a squab breast and set on a plate. Arrange a squab leg and a quail breast and leg beside it. Spoon some of the Persimmon Chutney around the plate and garnish with the radish sprouts.

* Garam masala is a blend of dry-roasted Indian spices, available at Indian markets.

* Sugar cane is a pure form of sugar, which is often in a cake form and available at specialty stores.

Jesse Perez

Chef, Francesca's at Sunset, at the Westin La Cantera
San Antonio, Texas

Wen I read a recipe, I can tell a lot about the author and designer of the dish. The spices and techniques chefs use and the amount of exuberance—a.k.a. intensity and effort—that goes into making a dish often reveal what part of the country they're from, how much training they've had, and even how old their age. When I first read Jesse Perez's recipe for venison chili, I could make good guesses about all-of-the-above—and then one more thing: I knew he was not just creative, but a maverick, an exciting and innovative wild chef.

Born and bred in San Antonio, Texas, Jesse first worked his way through college "flipping burgers" and making nachos.

"When I was at the University of Michigan, I entered all the chili contests," Jesse explained. "I'd get my mother in San Antonio to send me up the right chile peppers and spices. I came in first, twice."

Eventually Jesse moved to a fine-dining restaurant, where he first bussed and then asked if he could cook. In 1999, Jesse graduated with a degree in education and returned to San Antonio to find a job, not as a teacher, but as a chef.

Jesse started at the Westin La Cantera, working at several of the hotel's four restaurants under the tutelage of executive chef John Northcutt. In 2000, Jesse progressed to Westin's premier Francesca's at Sunset, where the celebrity chef Mark Miller is a consultant to the Francesca staff. Chef Miller is considered to be a culinary master of Southwestern cuisine and also is chef/owner of the well known Coyote Cafes in Sante Fe, New Mexico, and Las Vegas.

"Since we get to work alongside him, we really learn everything about this cuisine," Jesse said. "When we took a trip to Broken Arrow Ranch in Ingrid, Texas [a Mark Miller-endorsed venison purveyor, one of the very few that can supply free-range yet inspected deer meat to restaurants], I was inspired to create my venison chili. And it has become a very popular 'special' on the Francesca's menu. The venison isn't ground but cut into 1/2-inch cubes to maintain the integrity of the venison and not lose any of the flavor. I use toasted cumin and coriander seeds, then grind them. And also toasted Mexican oregano—key word is 'toasted'—because the toasting releases the oils and makes a whole new flavor element. I serve the chili with a fresh sweet corn tamale and cilantro crème fraîche so there is the contrast of sweet with spice. There's really a lot going on in this chili."

The blending and careful choice of ingredients in the Perez venison chili—from the good local dark beer, the Mexican cinnamon (canela), guajillo chile pepper to, of course, the Texas venison—make this recipe not just well conceived but give the region's distinct and robust flavors center stage. Yet in the state that claims to be the birthplace of chili and very nearly considers it a crime to add beans to chili, Perez's chili surprises by including black beans. It's definitely an out-of-the-box move.

"Black beans add to the presentation, and they are part of the Southwestern tradition here at Francesca's," Jesse said. "I used beans, all different kinds of beans, in my chili in Michigan—everyone from home thought I was crazy. But hey, I won!"

In the year since Jesse gave me his Maverick Venison Chili recipe, he's won a great deal more than chili contests. He won the *SAVEUR* Texas Hill Country Food & Wine Festival for best dish and best presentation with his Dijon buffalo rib-eye tamale dish. And he was the grand prize winner at San Antonio's Top Ten Chefs cook-off and fundraiser to benefit the March of Dimes.

Jesse continues to work with Mark Miller, whose input Jesse finds invaluable—and never overbearing.

"He lets me be experimental at Francesca's and try new dishes on the menu," Jesse said. "That's unusual for a celebrity chef."

Chile-Rubbed Grilled Rack of Texas Axis Venison with Pecan Wild Rice Pilaf, Tobacco Onion Rings, and Cascabel-Huckleberry Essence

(SERVES 4)

4 racks of Texas axis venison (10 ounces each, 4 bone rack portion)
Kosher salt
Freshly ground black pepper
8 tablespoons Axis Rub (see recipe below)
12 ounces Pecan Wild Rice Pilaf (see recipe below)
4 ounces Cascabel-Huckleberry Essence (see recipe below)
8 ounces Tobacco Onion Rings (see recipe below)

Thoroughly season each axis rack with salt and pepper and let sit for 30 minutes at room temperature.

Preheat the grill. When the grill is hot and ready, place the axis racks loin side down and cross mark on grill for 5 minutes. (It is best to eat axis venison at medium-rare, so to achieve, continue to cook in the oven.)

Preheat the oven to 425 degrees. Transfer the axis rack to a baking dish and bake in the preheated oven for 7 to 8 minutes until slightly firm to touch. Let the cooked axis rack sit for an additional 3 minutes to allow plating to take place. Layer Axis Rub (see recipe below) onto the loin portion of the axis racks.

Prepare the Pecan Wild Rice Pilaf (see recipe below), Cascabel-Huckleberry Essence (see recipe below), and Tobacco Onion Rings (see recipe below).

On a large dinner plate, place Pecan Wild Rice Pilaf in center of plate and spoon around the Cascabel-Huckleberry Essence. Cut each axis rack into two-chop portions; place crosswise on top of the Pecan Wild Rice Pilaf with every intention to display some height for presentation. Top with a hefty portion of Tobacco Onion Rings and serve immediately.

■　■　■

Axis Rub

8 shallots
8 garlic cloves
2 tablespoons New Mexico chile powder
2 tablespoons ancho chile powder
2 tablespoons chile powder
1 tablespoon ground toasted coriander
1 tablespoon ground toasted cumin
1 tablespoon black pepper
1 1/2 cups brown sugar
3 tablespoons kosher salt

Place the shallots and garlic in a food processor and blend till it forms a thick paste. (It is important that the garlic and shallots form a paste, so if you need to, add a couple drops of water to help.)

In a large mixing bowl, place the shallot-garlic paste with all the dry ingredients. Incorporate thoroughly to form a slightly thick paste. (Add more drops of water to thin out if necessary.)

. . .

Pecan Wild Rice Pilaf

2 tablespoons olive oil

1/4 cup finely chopped red bell pepper

1/4 cup finely chopped yellow bell pepper

1/4 cup finely chopped poblano chile pepper

1/4 cup roasted corn kernels (roasted corn-on-cob on the grill or frozen or canned corn, roasted in a frying pan with a drop of oil)

3 cups cooked wild rice (3/4 cup uncooked, cooked in chicken stock preferably)

3 cups cooked basmati rice (1 cup uncooked, cooked in chicken stock preferably)

1/4 cup roasted pecan pieces

Salt

Pepper

Heat the oil in a large sauté pan on high heat. Sauté all peppers and corn until soft, about 1 to 2 minutes. Add both wild rice and basmati rice and mix well to incorporate all ingredients. Add a couple of table-spoons of chicken stock to help with heating the overall mixture. Add pecans to wild rice and basmati rice mixture and season with salt and pepper. Keep warm.

. . .

Cascabel-Huckleberry Essence

2 pounds cascabel chiles

3 quarts boiling hot water

3 shallots, sliced

1 garlic clove, sliced

1 yellow onion, sliced

1 tablespoon olive oil

3 cloves

1/2 teaspoon allspice

1 tablespoon ground Mexican cinnamon (canela) or substitute regular cinnamon

1 tablespoon ground toasted coriander

1 tablespoon ground toasted cumin

1 quart cheap port wine

1 1/2 pounds frozen huckleberries, thawed

1 cup sugar

Preheat the oven to 375 degrees. Place the cascabel chiles on a sheet pan and bake in the preheated oven for 1 to 2 minutes until aromatic. (This process softens the chiles and rehydrates them to make them more pliable to de-seed. Do not leave chiles unattended, one minute more could over-toast chiles, which will make them bitter.)

De-seed each chile and discard the stems. Place the chiles in a large saucepot with boiling water and let cook for 15 minutes until very soft.

Remove the softened chiles from water and place in a high-speed blender. Puree the chiles till a thick paste forms. (If the chiles do not break down easily, add the some of the reserved water to thin out. Pass through a fine whole sieve and reserve the cascabel paste).

In a medium to large saucepan, sauté the shallots, garlic, and onion in the oil until carmelized. Lower the heat, add the cloves, allspice, canela, coriander, and cumin, and continue to cook until very aromatic and all ingredients come together to resemble a paste. Deglaze the saucepan with the wine and turn up the heat to bring to a boil. Add 1 pound of the huckleberries to the wine along with the sugar. Let the mixture boil for 10 minutes, or until it can coat the back of a spoon.

Transfer the reduced mixture to a high-speed blender and add the remaining 1/2 pound of huckleberries. Blend till emulsified and sweeten with more sugar if it is too tart. Add the reserved cascabel paste and blend for an additional minute till fully incorporated. If the mixture gets too thick, thin out with more port until smooth.

■   ■   ■

Tobacco Onion Rings

2 cups flour
2 tablespoons kosher salt
2 tablespoons black pepper
2 tablespoons New Mexico chile powder
1 tablespoon cayenne
2 yellow onions, thinly sliced
Salt
Pepper

Place the flour, salt, pepper, chile powder, and cayenne in a large mixing bowl and mix thoroughly. Add the onions to the seasoned flour and toss lightly to coat all of the onion.

Fry the onions in a fryer set at 350 degrees till golden brown. Season with salt and pepper to taste.

Maverick Venison Chili

(SERVES 8)

1/2 cup Spanish olive oil

2 1/4 pounds venison loin, cut into 1/2-inch cubes

Freshly ground black pepper

Kosher salt

2 poblano chiles, chopped

2 cups chopped Spanish yellow onion

2 leeks, chopped

2 serrano chile peppers, chopped

4 garlic cloves, minced

1/4 cup (or 1 1/2 tablespoons for a milder chili) Guajillo chile powder

2 tablespoons Mexican oregano, toasted

2 tablespoons coriander seeds, toasted and ground

2 tablespoons cumin, toasted and ground

1 teaspoon ground Mexican cinnamon (canela) or regular cinnamon
   can be substituted

1 bottle of Shiner Bock beer or other dark beer

4 cups chicken stock

2 cups black beans, cooked al dente

10 fire-roasted Roma tomatoes, roughly chopped

4 tablespoons chipotle puree

2 scallions, chopped (optional)

Add 1/4 cup of the oil in a large saucepan and heat. Season the venison generously with pepper and salt. Add the seasoned venison in small
batches to the saucepan, brown, and set aside, keeping all natural juices

in saucepot. Add the poblano chile peppers, onion, leeks, serrano chile peppers, and garlic. Sauté all vegetables over a low heat until tender.

Add the remaining 1/4 cup oil to saucepan and add the chile powder, oregano, coriander, cumin, and canela. Add the venison to the saucepan and coat the meat well with all the ingredients. After completely incorporating all ingredients, deglaze with the beer. Reduce the beer until it is almost gone and add the stock, beans, tomatoes, and chipotle puree.

Cover and simmer for 1 1/4 to 2 hours until the venison is fork tender. Check for seasoning. Garnish the chili with scallions, if using.

Serve the chile with sweet corn tamale and cilantro crème fraîche.

Coriander-Rubbed Loin of Antelope with Roasted Corn Waffles and Blackberry Sauce

(SERVES 4)

4 loin cuts of antelope (8 ounces each)
Salt
Pepper
Oil
8 tablespoons Coriander Rub (see recipe below)
4 tablespoons minced shallots
4 teaspoons minced garlic
8 tablespoons red wine
4 cups baby arugula
8 ounces Roasted Corn Waffle Batter (see recipe below)
8 ounces foie gras
8 ounces Blackberry Sauce (see recipe below)
Fresh chives (for garnish)

Preheat the oven to 450 degrees. Season the antelope with salt and pepper. In a sauté pan over medium heat, sear the antelope in the oil on all sides and place in the preheated until it reaches the preferred temperature, 120 degrees for rare, about 20 minutes. After the preferred temperature has been met, take the antelope out of the oven and let it sit for 5 minutes. At that time, rub the Coriander Rub (see recipe below) over the antelope.

Sauté shallots and garlic in more of the oil until aromatic, and then deglaze with the wine. After most of the moisture has evaporated, add and lightly wilt the arugula, being sure to maintain the character and color. Meanwhile, place Roasted Corn Waffle Batter (see recipe below) in a waffle maker and bake to order.

Slice the foie gras into 2-ounce portions. Season with salt and pepper. In a sauté pan over high heat, sear the foie gras on both sides until lightly golden brown. (Be sure not to overcook or scorch the foie gras.)

To assemble, spoon some Blackberry Sauce (see below) around the center of each dinner plate and place sautéed arugula in the middle. Cut the antelope loin on a bias to showcase temperature, and place crosswise on top of the arugula. Place a waffle on one side of antelope and top the waffle with seared foie gras. Garnish with fresh chives.

■   ■   ■

Coriander Rub

1/2 cup ground coriander
1/2 cup ground cumin
1/2 cup ground black pepper
1 cup brown sugar
2 tablespoons minced garlic
4 tablespoons minced shallots
1 tablespoon salt

Mix all ingredients in a mixing bowl. If the mixture needs more liquid, add just a few drops of water.

■   ■   ■

Roasted Corn Waffle Batter

1 cup flour
1/2 cup cornmeal
1 cup roasted corn kernels (roasted corn-on-cob on the grill or frozen
    or canned, roasted in a frying pan with a drop of oil)
1 tablespoon baking powder
2 cups buttermilk
4 eggs
1 teaspoon salt
2 tablespoons sugar

Mix all dry ingredients well. Incorporate dry mixture with all wet ingredients until a thick batter consistency has developed. Let sit for 20 minutes. Bake in a waffle iron.

■ ■ ■

Blackberry Sauce

1 cup reduced port wine
2 cloves
1 stick Mexican cinnamon (canela) or substitute a regular cinnamon
    stick
3 whole allspice berries
2 juniper berries
4 shallots, sliced
1 garlic clove, sliced
2 cups blackberry puree

Place all in small saucepot and bring to a simmer. Let simmer for 25 minutes until desired consistency then strain through cheesecloth. Let cool for 20 minutes before plating. Should be served at room temperature.

Jim Powell

Executive Chef and Owner, Gibson's Restaurant
Grand Rapids, Michigan

I came across Jim Powell and his wonderful foods when I was doing an article for *Field and Stream* magazine on the best recipes for venison stew, burgers, and chili—those basic venison recipes that you want to keep coming back to. Jim's Harvest Venison Stew fit the bill and came highly recommended to me by a trusted friend and good outdoorsman. (Well, as trusted has any walleye fishing buddy can be.) In addition to my friend's strong recommendation, Jim had another thing going for him that I knew would speak to the core of my wild culinary sensibilities: He is from Michigan.

There is in all of us a baseline of food memories that harbor not only what we perceive as good tasting, but often make up our own set of comfort foods. With 20 years of my childhood spent weekending and vacationing at our second home on the shores of the "the big lake," I was a sucker for Jim's recipes. He keyed off local and seasonal ingredients, those earthy flavors of a north county—autumn's root vegetables, the wild taste of morel mushrooms, brook trout, venison, and wild turkey. That all resonated, not only with a past but with a present and, I hoped always, a future me. And they clearly were foods Jim had spent time perfecting.

"I grew up as one of ten children in a hunting family where dishes that called for basically free meat, used virtually all cuts—even the lesser ones— and that would feed multitudes were an everyday necessity. We ate everything, woodcock and brook trout, and kept beagles for hunting rabbit. But I think I was around eight years old when I ate my first deer meat," Jim recalls. "It was cooked well-done and I remember I didn't like it very much. My dad cooked it—he cooked all the game. My mother really didn't ever cook game, or even have much of a chance to be a very good cook with so many children in the house, at least until later when half of us moved out and she could spend time on it. So by the time I was fourteen, I was working in the kitchen of a Grand Rapids steakhouse."

Working in a series of restaurants, Jim picked up a range of kitchen skills. From the Grand Rapids steakhouse butcher who'd been with the Dutch underground in World War II, Jim learned traditional European-style techniques for aging and cutting meat. Jim apprenticed in the Sonoma region of California with *Cordon Bleu*–trained chef Perry Taylor and returned to Grand Rapids to work in a series of corporate and executive chef positions until he opened Gibson's in 1983. On occasion Jim also gives game cooking seminars—focusing on braising techniques or game bird preparation—at local hunting clubs.

"The front shoulder/leg of a deer makes for choice—flavorful and tender—stew meat and requires less cooking than the typically-used neck meat, which tends to be tough," Jim said. "If you don't know what cut the butcher used to make the stew meat, the age or size of the deer [older and bigger tends also to be tough], the safest plan is to cook the stew longer. But be careful to add more liquid so the stewing sauce doesn't get too concentrated. Water or more Zinfandel can be added. I use a red Zinfandel because it is a lighter wine but with plenty of spice and depth to it."

When I tested Jim's recipe for venison stew, I ended up adding quite a bit more Zinfandel and water and adjusting the recipe—increasing the amount of liquids called for to what you see on page 200. Jim was surprised at the need for more, but he realized that in converting his restaurant recipe—which made literally gallons of venison stew—to family-size proportions, well, something got lost in the translation. (The recipe conversion conundrum is common for chefs, but it provides us food writers with job security.) And certainly once we made the change, the stew was absolutely sublime.

A year later, I spoke with Jim about adding more recipes to his section of this book and asked for an update. The restaurant business was good and getting better with the improving economy, but Jim said that he had been thinking more and more of retiring—maybe in a few years or so—and he'd been considering maybe having a smaller restaurant, with only seventy to eighty seats. That, he confessed, was truly his dream.

"It would be so much fun, so much less stressful and I could really cook," Jim said.

How true, I thought. Just think how much easier Jim's life would be by down-sizing from the gallon-size restaurant, lounge, catering, banquet, wedding, dinner, and lunch business at Gibson's to an intimate, small eatery. And just think of all those recipes that would need conversion, all that testing, and all that eating of fabulous food. I'm thinking this could be the start of a wonderful relationship.

Harvest Venison Stew

(SERVES 8)

2 cups canned beef consommé

2 cups red Zinfandel

2 tablespoons tomato paste

3/4 cup water

2 ounces smoked-dried morels or dried morels with 1/4 teaspoon
    Wright Liquid smoke

2 tablespoons olive oil

2 pounds venison (preferably from the front shoulder or upper leg),
    cubed into 3/4-inch cubes

1/4 pounds chopped bacon

4 tablespoons chopped shallots

2 tablespoons chopped fresh garlic

1/2 cup rutabaga, cubed into 3/4-inch cubes

1/2 cup parsnip, cubed into 3/4-inch cubes

1/2 cup turnip, cubed into 3/4-inch cubes

1/2 cup yam, cubed into 3/4-inch cubes

4 tablespoons flour

In a saucepan, combine the consommé, Zinfandel, tomato paste, water, morels (and liquid smoke if using just dried morels) and simmer over low heat for about 20 minutes.

Heat a skillet or Dutch oven over medium-high heat, add the oil and brown the venison cubes on all sides. Remove the venison from the skillet. Add the bacon to the skillet to brown. Pour off most of the rendered fat and add the shallots and garlic to the bacon bits and sauté briefly.

Add the rutabaga, parsnip, turnip, and yam, brown slightly, sprinkle with flour, and stir. Add the venison and the re-constituted morel mixture, reduce the heat, and let simmer on low approximately for 45 minutes or until venison is tender. (If using an older deer or tougher cuts of venison, cooking time should be doubled, to approximately 1 1/2 hours, adding 1/2 cup water if necessary.)

Serve with a crusty, hearty, toasted rye bread and salad.

Fresh Brook Trout with Crushed Hazelnuts and Fine Herb Butter

(SERVES 4)

Flour

2 brook trout or small rainbow trout, butterflied and dressed (approximately 8 ounces each)

2 ounces neutral cooking oil (such as safflower or peanut)

1/2 cup crushed hazelnuts

3 ounces chicken stock

1 tablespoon fresh lime juice or lemon juice

1 ounce dry white wine

3 ounces Fine Herb Butter (see recipe below), softened

Use a large enough skillet or nonstick pan to give the fish enough room. Dust the fish lightly with flour and shake off any excess. Heat the pan over medium high heat and add the oil. Place the fish flesh side down in the pan and cook until golden brown. Turn and cook another 2 minutes. Remove the fish to warm platter.

Dump the excess oil from the pan and add the hazelnuts, toasting briefly. Now add the lime or lemon juice, wine, and stock and reduce the mixture by half over medium heat. Reduce the heat to low and add the Fine Herb Butter (see recipe below). Incorporate the butter using a wire whisk (The sauce should have a creamy texture; do not boil it or it will break.) Pour the Fine Herb Butter over the trout and serve immediately.

• • •

Fine Herb Butter

2 ounces finely chopped shallots
2 tablespoons fresh chopped tarragon
2 tablespoons fresh chopped parsley
2 tablespoons fresh chopped chives
1 pound lightly salted butter, softened

Sauté the shallots briefly until wilted. Combine the shallots and herbs with the butter. Roll the butter into a tube-wrap in parchment, then plastic wrap and refrigerate or freeze. Slice coin-size slices to melt over vegetables or roasted fish or soften for cooking.

Braised Pheasant Chasseur with Sausage Stuffed Pheasant Leg

(SERVES 4)

1 pheasant, quartered (2 1/2–3 pounds)

1 egg white

1/2 cup fresh basil leaves

1 teaspoon crushed garlic

1/4 cup heavy cream

1/2 teaspoon black pepper

1 cup chopped bacon

1 tablespoon butter

2 tablespoons flour (plus extra for dredging pheasant breasts)

1 cup finely chopped shiitake mushrooms

1 cup mirepoix of carrot, celery, and white onion, finely chopped

3 cups game stock or beef stock

2 cups red wine (Pinot Noir or Merlot)

1/4 cup tomato paste

Olive oil

Kosher salt

Black pepper

Remove the breast bones from the pheasant breast and save the bones for stock. Leaving the skin attached at the small end of the drumstick, gently peel down the skin of the legs and thighs. Cut around the drumstick bone (above the pulled back skin) and remove thigh and leg meat.

Set aside the meat from both drumsticks and thighs for making sausage. Using the backside of a chef's knife, cut the bone off above the skin, saving the bones for stock.

In a food processor, combine the thigh and leg meat, egg white, basil, garlic, cream, pepper, and half of the bacon. Using the blade attachment, pulse until the mixture resembles breakfast sausage. Stuff the sausage mixture into the leg skin and reshape to resemble the thigh and leg. Set aside.

Heat a heavy gauge sauté pan or Dutch oven with lid. Melt the butter. Dust the pheasant breasts with flour and brown on both sides. Remove the breasts and set aside. Add the remaining half of the bacon to the pan or Dutch oven and lightly brown. Add the mushrooms and sauté until partially cooked, add the mirepoix and cook until the celery and onions start to become translucent. Sprinkle with 2 tablespoons of flour and stir. Add stock, wine, and tomato paste. Mix together. Put the browned pheasant breasts back into this mixture and bring to a simmer. Continue to simmer for approximately 30 minutes.

While the pheasant breasts are cooking, preheat the oven to 375 degrees. Grease a cookie sheet with the oil. Brush the "sausage legs" with the oil. Sprinkle lightly with salt and pepper. Roast for approximately 20 minutes. After the legs have cooked, let them rest at least 5 minutes. They can then be served with the breasts as is or may be sliced for a nicer presentation.

Notes: Serve with grilled vegetables and whole roasted potatoes. If you do not want to tackle making the sausage, legs and thighs can be skinned, seasoned, and roasted for 45 minutes in a 350 degree oven. Now the legs and thighs can be added to the breasts for the 30 minute simmer.

Roast Wild Turkey in Honey Brine

(SERVES ABOUT 4)*

1 whole wild turkey, plucked and cleaned
3 quarts boiling water
8 bay leaves
8 cloves
1/2 cup whole black peppercorns
1/4 cup smoked sweet paprika
1 head garlic, halved
2 teaspoons cayenne
1 cup kosher or sea salt
2 cups honey
1/2 cup sugar
1 bottle inexpensive Riesling (semi-dry)
Pan Gravy (see recipe below)

In a large roasting pan, pour the boiling water over the bay leaves, cloves, peppercorns, paprika, garlic, cayenne, salt, honey, and sugar and whisk to dissolve salt and sugar completely. Allow the mixture to steep until at room temperature, then add Riesling.

Immerse the whole turkey in the brine for at least 4 hours. If not totally immersed, turn the bird a few times. If a whole bird is not available, reduce the time in the brine to 2 1/2 hours.

Preheat the oven to 350 degrees. Place the bird in a cooking bag and roast it in the preheated oven for approximately 20 minutes per pound (if the bird weighs 8 pounds or less, about 15 minutes per pound) if it's in the 15-pound range. Reserve the juices from the cooking bag to make Pan Gravy (see recipe below).

. . .

Pan Gravy

Reserved juices from cooking bag
Chicken stock
2 tablespoons dark Karo syrup
1 tablespoon tomato paste
Roux or cornstarch (optional)

Pour the reserved juices from the cooking bag into a heavy saucepan. Skim the fat (there should be little) and add the stock (if necessary) to make 1 quart. Add the Karo syrup and tomato paste and simmer for 30 minutes. This may be thickened with roux or cornstarch or served au jus.

Wild turkey range widely in weight, depending on the age, sex, and season they're taken. For determining number of servings from the turkey, figure 1 to 1 1/2 pounds per person.

Priscilla Martel and Charlie van Over

Chefs, Cookbook Authors, and Food Consultants
Chester, Connecticut

"Who *are* these chefs?" I queried my in-laws who were taking us out to dinner in Chester, Connecticut. It was the early 1980s when I was in the habit of evaluating the quality of a restaurant based on the virtues—or lack thereof—in the butter, bread, and crème brûlée. I was well into my second slice from a fantastically flavorful, crusty, baguette—complete with fat pats of sweet butter—and listening to the waiter recite the evening specials. With entrees and appetizers that included venison, rabbit, pheasant, duck—so much game, and in era when U.S. restaurants rarely offered it—my food gauge was clearly way too rudimentary for this place. My bar for restaurant excellence was ratcheting skyward by the minute. It seemed obvious to me that the couple doing the cooking at this restaurant must have been born into that world where daily attention and devotion to food—so intrinsic to European cultures—is patiently practiced. They must be French, with extensive training in France. Years later I would learn I was wrong.

Charlie van Over and Priscilla Martel—the owners, chefs and co-creators of Restaurant du Village—had both grown up, been educated in the United States and never attended formal culinary school anywhere. I met them when Priscilla was writing a cookbook and long after they sold the restaurant to

Michel and Cynthia Keller (see pages 74). The sale of their wonderful brain-child was made palatable at least in part because Charlie and Priscilla knew that despite the Connecticut address the true feel they'd created of "a family-owned restaurant in rural France" would naturally be maintained by the French-born Michel Keller.

Priscilla and Charlie may not have been born in France, but what they did each have was a childhood legacy of culinary experiences, which created a well-formulated and refined palate. Priscilla's grandmothers—one Polish the other French—along with her mother, simply always cooked and baked, mentoring her as a little girl in the family's regard for cooking and food. It seemed only natural when Priscilla went off to college for her to initiate a food co-op—coordinating, planning, and many times cooking nightly meals for the 30 or 40 students at the French House at Brown University. During that same time, Priscilla met Charlie, and they started first a catering business, and then in 1978 they opened a small restaurant in Essex, Connecticut, called the Flying Scotsman.

Charlie grew up on Long Island—with ready access to the cosmopolitan food influences of New York city—and started experimenting with cooking at the age of ten. His culinary development, however, was not solely derived from city sophistication. With grandparents living in rural Pennsylvania and ancestry that could be traced to famed shooters Buffalo Bill and Texas Jack, Charlie came naturally to hunting, recalling woodchuck as his first quarry. Clearly woodchuck wouldn't have contributed much to cultivating anyone's taste for game, although Charlie says since then he has prepared very tasty woodchuck. His hunting and culinary focus did quickly turn to upland birds.

Charlie went to Johns Hopkins University and thought he wanted to be a screenwriter, but he always cooked for his college friends and professors and did food consulting. In 1976, Charlie joined a retail-consulting company and convinced the company to expand into the restaurant and food retail market-place, developing such projects as the Market at Citicorp Center in Manhattan.

But by 1978, the partnership of Priscilla and Charlie and their combined passion for cooking would lead them to open Restaurant du Village. Like an East Coast conceptual sister to Alice Waters' Berkeley restaurant, Chez Pannise, they sought out local farmers for the very freshest produce and used only fish caught regionally and, like Waters, maintained a very seasonal menu. Charlie, of course, made certain locally raised game was available, too. The restaurant sponsored an annual shooting event at a nearby hunting preserve for guest chefs and initiated a Festival Diane (Roman Goddess of the Hunt) food theme for the du Village menu in late fall.

Charlie explained, "Everything has its season: trout in the spring, striped bass in the summer, tomatoes in August—that's when they should be eaten— and game is the very spirit of the fall season."

Priscilla joined in, "Game is a leading player on the stage of culinary art, it has such a personality and dimension of character. . ."

Charlie enthusiastically interrupted, "There's a pronounced purity in wild game. Your job as the cook is to determine how best to release the flavor, not mask it, to bring out the distinct wildness. . ."

Priscilla was trying to interject herself back into the discussion, but Charlie was on a roll, "Game stands on its own two feet."

I thought about pointing out that it sometimes stands on four feet, then thought better of it and redirected the discussion to what is their favorite game bird to cook.

"Woodcock," Charlie said unhesitatingly. "Rare. And remember there is no such thing in game cooking as medium rare. It's either overcooked or it's rare."

Priscilla was just as definite with her response, "Squab, too, those nice dark meats," she answered, paused and then chuckled. "But you remember, don't you, Charlie? That time I cooked woodcock for you at the restaurant, the time when I redefined the concept of 'cleaning' a game bird?"

Charlie professed not to remember. "Charlie'd come into the restaurant after a day of woodcock hunting and had two birds," Priscilla explained. "I plucked them, left each bird in the round, seared them quickly, and set them aside while Charlie finished his appetizer, holding them on a searing platter. The birds awaited the finishing of their cooking amongst several similar 'used' platters. I'm certain it never occurred to the little dishwasher girl that the plat-ter wasn't set there to be washed. So the birds were plunged into a sink full of soapy, warm water. Fortunately it was only moments before I realized my woodcock had disappeared and could rescue them from their Palmolive bath. And since they were whole, intact, and seared properly, they didn't really get overexposed to the detergent. So I completed the cooking process and served them. And they were good. Right, Charlie?"

"I don't remember any of this," Charlie sounded a bit aghast. "But since I don't remember it, it must mean they were fine."

I thought it certainly was good that Priscilla's searing technique was well-developed and skilled. Not only did it seal in the meat's juices, as is intended with searing, but it clearly sealed out the soap, too.

Wanting to move on, Charlie and Priscilla sold Restaurant du Village to Michel and Cynthia Keller in 1990. Priscilla then became executive chef at the Norwich Inn & Spa in Connecticut, working to develop healthful, "Spa" recipes. Then, as now, both Charlie and Priscilla devote much of their time to their food consulting business, All About Food, with their abundant client list ranging from the Idaho Potato Commission and Absolut Vodka to Cuisinart and the Parrish Art Museum.

In addition, Charlie has pursued his interest in bread baking and, with Priscilla, wrote *The Best Bread Book Ever*, Broadway Books (1997) which won both the IACP Julia Child Award and the James Beard Award. Charlie actually holds a U.S. patent on his bread mixing and baking technologies.

Well, I was wrong about them being French and the formal training. I may now use olive oil instead of butter, and even I can make a great crème brûlée. But I did know—from those two great harbingers of culinary excellence, perfect bread, perfect game birds—that something exceptional was happening at Restaurant du Village. Who *are* these chefs? Two who know how to nourish not just the body but the soul. It's in the bread; it's in the game.

Poor Man's Rich Stock, Mushroom Variation

(MAKES APPROXIMATELY 1 QUART REDUCED STOCK)

3 pounds or more pheasant or chicken bones, raw and/or left over from roasting, including hearts and gizzards

2 medium carrots, peeled and chopped

2 stalks celery, chopped coarse

2 medium onions, skin on, chopped coarse

2 ounces dried mushrooms (morels, porcini, shiitake, or any field mushrooms you may have gathered and dried) ground to a powder in a blender, food processor, or small coffee grinder.

1 small head garlic, halved crosswise, skin on

10 black peppercorns

3 bay leaves

5 sprigs parsley

1/4 teaspoon dried thyme

1/2 teaspoon dried tarragon

3 ounces tomato paste

1 pig's foot

3 quarts or more cold water (enough to cover all the above ingredients)

Place all the ingredients in a 6 to 8-quart saucepan or stockpot. Add additional water to cover all ingredients. Bring to a boil then reduce heat and simmer for at least 3 hours. Check each hour and add more water, if needed, to keep the ingredients covered. Drain the stock, reserving the liquid and discarding the bones. Return the stock to the pan and reduce over medium heat to approximately 1 quart. This concentrated stock may be cooled and refrigerated or frozen where it will keep for a couple of months. Use undiluted to make rich sauces. Dilute with equal parts water to use when making risotto or soups.

We can't live without some sort of game/poultry stock in our freezer and find it a good use for pheasant carcasses. In order to make this stock recipe, you need to have saved the bones from chickens and/or game birds for a game stock. I also buy whole chickens whenever we use chicken. The bones that go into the stock are usually a combination of raw trimmings and carcasses from whole roasted birds. Simply stash them in the freezer in plastic bags until you have accumulated three or more pounds. . . enough to fill a 6-quart saucepan three quarters the way up. This stock when reduced to a thick gelatinous consistency may be stored in the freezer.* It's the basic 'glace de viande' and the secret of many chefs for creating great flavors in many meat and game dishes.

The secret of the stock is quite simple. With the addition of the tomato paste, you get the sauce to darken without any tomato flavor and with the addition of the pig's foot, you get the gelatinous consistency without any pork flavor. If you happen to be cooking kosher you can substitute granulated or sheet gelatin, which is available in most markets.

For a strong mushroom flavor, dried mushrooms will give the best results. We usually dry at least half of the mushrooms we harvest and use them all winter long.

*As you read this book you come to see certain constants in good game cooking. Making your own game stock is one of those constants. When I freeze stock, I do so in ice cube trays (I also do this with pesto) and once frozen dump the stock cubes into a plastic bag to keep in the freezer. This makes it easy to store and to use varying portions without having to freeze and un-freeze a large container full of stock.

Wild Mushroom Risotto

(SERVES 4)

6–10 ounces fresh wild mushrooms
1 ounce dry mushrooms, soaked in hot water for 30 minutes
2 tablespoons olive oil
2 tablespoons unsalted butter
1/4 cup finely minced shallots
Salt
Freshly ground black pepper
4–5 cups homemade stock
1 1/2 cups arborio rice
1 tablespoon butter
1/4–1/2 cup finely grated Parmigiano-Reggiano cheese
3 tablespoons black truffle juice (optional)

Trim the stems from the fresh mushrooms and set aside for stock or discard. Slice the mushrooms into thin slices. Cut large caps into 1-inch pieces if necessary. Reserve the soaking liquid from the dry mushrooms. Trim any tough bits from the dry mushrooms and discard. Set the mushrooms aside.

Heat the oil and the 2 tablespoons butter in a large saucepan. Add the shallots and cook over medium high heat until pale golden in color. Add the mushrooms and season with salt and pepper. Cook, stirring occasionally for another 6 to 10 minutes to release some of the mushroom juices.

While the mushrooms cook, bring the stock to a simmer in a separate pot.

Add the rice to the sautéed mushrooms and shallots and cook for approximately 5 minutes to slightly toast the grains. Increase the heat to high and add 1 cup of stock to the rice. Cook, stirring constantly, until most of the liquid is absorbed. Continue to add liquid, a cup at a time as needed, stirring until the risotto is tender but still chewy, approximately 20 minutes. Add water should additional liquid be needed.

Remove the risotto from the heat and stir in the 1 tablespoon butter and cheese. Season with more salt and pepper as needed. Stir in the truffle juice, if using.

We're fortunate to find a good variety of some of the more flavorful varieties of wild mushrooms right in our backyard. Boletus edulus, lactarius (good for texture), false chanterelles and true chanterelles appear at more or less the same time. When there is a bumper crop of many types, we dry them in a slow oven. Many varieties, such as Suillus (Slippery Jack), develop a more intense flavor when dried. A combination of fresh and dry varieties makes an aromatic risotto. The truffle juice is optional but really heightens the taste of this special dish. It is available from D'Artagnan's (see page 15).

Wood-Grilled Scottish Red-Legged Partridge with Red Wine, Herb, and Bacon Butter

(SERVES 4)

4 red-legged partridge, dressed
1/2 cup gin or Absolut Kurant Vodka
Red Wine, Herb, and Bacon Butter (see recipe below)
4 slices country bread, crusts removed
1 tablespoon butter, melted
1 tablespoon olive oil
Salt
Pepper
Vegetable oil
Watercress Salad with Mustard Vinaigrette (see recipe below)

Split the partridge down the back to flatten. Place in a shallow dish. Douse with the gin or vodka and cover with plastic wrap. Marinate for several hours at room temperature or overnight in the refrigerator.

While the birds marinate prepare the Red Wine, Herb, and Bacon Butter (see recipe below).

Finish the partridge by preparing a wood fire for grilling. The fire is ready when the flames have died down and all that remains are glowing embers. Brush the bread with a mixture of the butter and olive oil. Grill over the fire for about 2 minutes on each side or until bread has grill marks and is lightly toasted. Season with salt and pepper. Set aside.

Preheat the oven to 250 degrees. Pat the birds to dry them, brush lightly with the vegetable oil and season with salt and pepper. Place the birds on the grill, cut side down. Grill for about 7 to 10 minutes, turn and grill for another 5 minutes. (All this depends on the fire heat and the size of the birds. Use your judgment, making certain the birds are rare to medium rare.) Remove the birds from the fire and hold them in the preheated oven while you assemble the Watercress Salad with Mustard Vinaigrette (see recipe below).

To serve, toss the watercress with the dressing then divide the watercress between four dinner plates. Place each partridge slightly overlapping the salad. Top with two 1/4-inch slices of the Red Wine, Herb, and Bacon Butter.

• • •

Red Wine, Herb, and Bacon Butter

2–3 thick cut slices of bacon
1 small shallot, finely chopped, about a 1/4 cup
2 tablespoons dry red wine
1/2 teaspoon dry tarragon or 1 teaspoon fresh
2 teaspoons sea salt
About 10 grindings black pepper
4 ounces unsalted butter, cut into several pieces, at room temperature

Preheat the oven to 400 degrees and line a plate with a paper towel. Lay the bacon out onto a baking sheet and bake in the oven until thoroughly cooked crisp and crunchy, about 5 minutes. Transfer the cooked bacon onto the paper towel to drain and cool. While the bacon is cooling, place the shallot, wine, tarragon, salt, and pepper in the bowl of a small food processor. Process for a few seconds to blend and dissolve the salt. Add the butter. Process until well blended.

Chop the cooked bacon into 1/4-inch bits. Stir the bacon into the butter with a fork. Scrape the butter onto a sheet of plastic wrap. Form the butter into a short tube about 1-inch in diameter. Roll the butter up in the plastic wrap and store in the refrigerator until ready to serve the partridge.

. . .

Watercress Salad with Mustard Vinaigrette

1 plump bunch fresh watercress
2 tablespoons red wine vinegar
1 teaspoon prepared honey mustard
1/4 teaspoon salt
5–6 grinds pepper
3 tablespoons heavy cream
1 tablespoon vegetable oil

Trim the watercress stems about 1/2 inch before washing. Wash and pat the watercress dry. Place in the refrigerator until ready to serve. In a medium-size salad bowl, combine the vinegar, mustard, salt and pepper with a fork. Add the cream and oil and blend with a fork until slightly emulsified. Season with more salt and pepper if necessary. Add the watercress to the bowl and toss.

Index